Hammerin' Hank of the Braves

by JOEL H. COHEN

Illustrated with photographs

Cover: Wide World

SCHOLASTIC BOOK SERVICES

NEW YORK • TORONTO • LONDON • AUCKLAND • SYDNEY • TOKYO

To Ann, Harvey, Alan, and Ivan—and
everyone who loves the game as much
as the winning.

Copyright © 1971 by Henry Aaron and Joel H. Cohen. All rights
reserved. Published by Scholastic Book Services, a division of
Scholastic Magazines, Inc.

5th printing ....October 1973

Printed in the U.S.A.

Contents

Introduction: Countdown to Glory

714 — Every baseball fan knows the magic number. Babe Ruth reached that lifetime home-run record back in 1935. Thirty-five years later, experts were still saying the Babe's 714 record would never be challenged.

But by 1973, Henry Aaron, 39-year-old superstar of the Atlanta Braves, had chalked up 673 home runs. He needed only 41 more to tie Ruth; 42 for a new mark. The magic number was suddenly within reach!

As the 1973 season advanced, fans crossed their fingers and roared for another home run whenever Aaron stepped to the plate. And each time, he faced a pitcher who had one mission: to halt Hank.

A few die-hard baseball fans hoped that the Babe's 714 record would stand forever. But most fans cheered Hank on, begging him to belt one out of the park. TV and radio broadcasters and newspapers trumpeted the countdown as "Hammerin' Hank" slugged his way to the Babe's seemingly unbeatable record.

Aaron is called the "Hammer" by his teammates for the way he pounds out base hits, and "Bad Henry" by opposing hurlers for the way he manhandles their best pitches.

But home runs aren't Aaron's only claim to fame. Hank's whiplash wrists have put him near the top of every important lifetime hitting category. Among active players, Hank is number one in batting average — in hits, in extra-base hits, in runs batted in, in doubles, and, of course, home runs. The all-time leader in total bases, he is closing in on Willie Mays, among active players, as leader in games played and runs scored.

Aaron has been the National League's Most Valuable Player; he's led the league in batting, homers, and RBI's, and more than once has led in two of those departments in one season. He was the first player to connect for 3,000 hits and 500 homers.

Besides his hitting prowess, Hank is a good glove man with an accurate arm, an intelligent, heads-up player, and a fine base runner.

His appointment as captain of the Atlanta Braves was official recognition of his leadership value to the team, and for the way he encourages and helps young players.

But because his excellence is unspectacular and quiet, people know very little about him. Here are the important highlights of his life and accomplishments, and a sampling of the thoughts and opinions of Hammerin' Hank Aaron, superstar of baseball.

1

The Charmed Circle

HANK had wanted it to happen at home at Atlanta Stadium. Now, he just wanted it to happen.

"It" was the 3,000th base hit of his major-league career — the hit that, until then, had been reached by only seven other great hitters in the entire history of baseball.

He'd been dreaming about that 3,000th hit ever since his first big-league season sixteen years earlier, when he had gotten 131 rookie hits. This year, 1970, it looked like a sure thing. Somehow, though, the 3,000th was proving harder to get than any of the 2,999 safeties that had led up to it.

One Sunday afternoon in May 1970, Hank

Aaron determined to nail that hit he needed to join the charmed circle of Ty Cobb, Tris Speaker, Nap Lajoie, Eddie Collins, Honus Wagner, Paul Waner, and Stan Musial. He was playing a double-header at Crosley Field, the Cincinnati Reds' old ballpark, a place that held fond memories for him, for he had played his first major-league game there. So if he couldn't get the 3,000th hit at home, then let it happen at Crosley Field.

The park was packed that day — 36,217 fans, the largest crowd in nearly a quarter century, most of them there because they hoped to see Hank make his historic hit. The fans cheered wildly as Number 44 ambled toward the plate, leaned his bat against his leg, and adjusted his batting helmet. Then he dug in and menacingly waved his bat (which some writers have compared to the twitching tail of a panther about to pounce).

On the mound for the Reds was Jim Merritt. He was determined to avoid the dubious honor of being the man who served Hammerin' Hank Aaron his 3,000th hit. He challenged Aaron. He gave him pitches to hit, but kept him off-stride. All four times that Hank stepped to the plate, Merritt didn't try to walk him or pitch around him — and all four times, Hank was retired, grounding out

8

twice, flying out, and fanning. Frustration. Disappointment.

But there was still the second game to be played. Pressure mounting, Hank came up to the plate in the first inning to face rookie Wayne Simpson. The Reds' shift was on — three infielders between second and third base — to try to cut Aaron's power to pull to left, and perhaps entice him to try to punch to right. But Hank cut away, and rapped a grounder right through the middle. Woody Woodward managed to run over and stop the ball from going into the outfield, but Felix Millan, who had been on second, scored, and Henry legged it safely to first.

At last! He had his 3,000th hit, a distinction not even such greats as Ruth, Gehrig, Williams, and DiMaggio had earned. And he was now the first player in baseball history to have hit at least 500 home runs with that many safeties. (Willie Mays got his 3,000th hit later in the season.)

Play was stopped so that the history-making ball could be presented to Hank by Stan Musial, then the most recent player to become a member of the 3,000-hit club.

"Congratulations," said the former St. Louis Cardinal superstar. "It was a great thrill to see you do it."

Hank celebrates his 3,000th hit, with Stan Musial (left), one of the seven players before him to do it, and Bill Bartholomay, Braves' president.

"Thanks so much for coming," Henry replied. "I'm grateful you could be here."

Hall-of-Famer Musial had followed his own 3,000th hit with a homer his next time at bat. Wouldn't it be something if Hank could duplicate Stan the Man's feat?

In the third inning, Hank had his chance. With a man on base, Hank did follow *his* 3,000th hit with a two-run homer! Then he even topped that by igniting a three-run rally with a tenth inning single, to go three-for-five in the game.

It was a great day for him and for his teammates — great but not perfect, for the Braves lost the game in fifteen innings. It was their second defeat of the day.

Hank was of course mightily pleased — and relieved too — that he had made his long-sought hit. He kissed the ball for the photographers and happily accepted the congratulations of his team and its president, Bill Bartholomay. But he was really glum about the outcome of the game.

"It really felt good at the time," he said of his achievement, "but now, I don't know . . . not after we lost the game. That takes something away. . . ." His reaction underscored the kind of team player Hank has always been.

Collecting 3,000 hits was a phenomenal achievement, something within the reach of only a consistent hitter, enjoying many, many excellent seasons.

Hank Aaron's years of excellence started when he was just a boy with a tremendous passion for the game. . . .

2

Baseball in His Blood

"I LOVED baseball. Every chance I got, I was on the ballfield hitting a baseball or throwing or catching one. I really loved it."

This is Henry Louis Aaron's recollection of the delicious taste baseball gave him as a boy in Mobile, Alabama, where he was born on February 5, 1934, third of eight children.

"Baseball kind of grew up in my family," Henry said, "and I kind of grew up with it. . . . I guess it was in my blood."

Hank's father and uncle were very good ballplayers, and his three brothers (a fourth died of pneumonia at an early age) apparently also inherited the talent. Brother Tommie for a while was Hank's teammate on the

Braves; their older brother, Herbert, played well before Army service; and their younger brother, James, hopes to make baseball his career. In addition to these three baseball-minded brothers, Hank has three sisters: Sarah (Jones), Gloria (Robinson), and Alfredia (Scott).

His father, who now operates a grocery store Hank bought for him and Mrs. Aaron, was a rivet-bucker ("Whatever that is," Hank laughs.) for the Alabama Drydock and Shipbuilding Company, a job that sent him home exhausted. Many weeks he didn't make even a hundred dollars, which was not much, considering the large family he had to feed and clothe. There was usually enough to eat in the Aaron household, thanks mainly to a garden Henry's parents planted, and his hard-working father managed to leave Hank spending money every morning before his son left for high school. Henry shared a bed with his brother, his shoes had to last two years, and when Christmas came, some of the Aarons went without gifts.

Summers, to help earn money, Hank used to mow lawns, and, for a short time, became an ice-man. He would lug fifty-pound blocks of ice on his back up two or three flights of stairs.

When Hank was born, his family lived in a black section of Mobile called "Down the Bay," and later moved to Toulminville, another part of the city. Tommie Agee, Cleon Jones, Billy Williams, and Willie McCovey are also from the Mobile area.

Though Hank emphasizes that for the past ten years Mobile has been ahead of many cities in racial progress (Spring Hill College there has always been integrated), Hank spent his childhood in segregated neighborhoods, attending segregated schools and movie houses. His heroes? "Well, I suppose every black player has to name Jackie Robinson. He was mine," Hank said. "Of course, Ted Williams I always admired for his hitting ability. Stan Musial was the same way. Joe DiMaggio was another of my heroes. But of all these fellows, I would have to pick Jackie Robinson." Once, the Brooklyn Dodgers came to Mobile for an exhibition game and Hank had a chance to see Robinson, the first black man to play in the major leagues, perform.

Hank himself might have played with the Dodgers. They annually ran a tryout camp in Mobile, attracting hundreds of youngsters from all around. But the year that Hank went (the first time blacks were invited), someone told him, "You're too small to play baseball. Go back home," and Hank just left without trying out.

What kind of child was Henry? "One of the best you could find," according to his mother. She recalls that, except for ballplaying, he enjoyed being alone. "He'd run a mile to watch a ballgame," she said.

"I suppose you could say I was a lazy kid and a smart kid," Hank says. "I was lazy as far as doing chores around the house, but smart when it came to playing baseball and other sports. This is really what I wanted to do, even when I was eleven or twelve years old."

It was about then that Hank and his older brother, Herbert, helped their father build the family a house. They used wood taken from torn-down Army depots. One of Hank's jobs was to straighten the nails he pulled out of the old boards.

In the new house, one of Hank's chores was to cut wood for the family's stove. The rule was no ballplaying until he had filled his quota of wood. More than once, Hank confesses, he'd secretly place some of his unchopped wood in his brother's pile, so he could get out to play sooner. On the other hand, Henry was so eager to get ballgames started, he'd even help friends finish *their* chores, so they could come out and play.

He was a quiet boy, and never really gave his parents trouble. And all it took to make him happy was a baseball game. Hank would spend hours and hours playing, and supper was about the only thing that could lure him away. He was a youngster with a big appetite.

Sometimes, after dark, Henry would practice by hitting soda-pop tops with a broomstick under the street light in a game that had boundaries marked off for singles, extra-base hits, outs, etc.

When he wasn't playing baseball or variations of it, he read about the sport every chance he had and he listened to games on radio or watched on TV.

A game he desperately wanted to listen to was the one to decide the 1951 pennant between the then New York Giants and Brooklyn Dodgers. Bitter rivals always, they had tied for first place in the National League and each had won a game of their three-game play-off.

The trouble was, it was a school day. Hank wouldn't have been permitted to miss school to listen at home. The one place in town where he *could* listen without anyone bringing up the fact that he should be in school was the poolroom, and that's where he spent the afternoon. The game had one of the most memorable finishes in baseball history — Bobby Thomson's three-run homer in the bottom of the ninth to bring the Giants back from the edge of defeat, and win them the pennant. It would always remain with Hank as the prime example of an important home run.

Unfortunately, Hank's father came home early from work that day. He made a surprise visit to the poolroom and discovered his hooky-playing son. The scolding that followed wasn't too severe since Mr. Aaron realized how important baseball was to Hank. But he felt there was enough free time after school to enjoy it. "My father was not an educated man," Hank recalls, "but he still knew the value of an education. He wanted me to get one." As a matter of fact, Hank (who now feels as strongly about the importance of education as his father) almost didn't accept an offer to play pro ball because his father wanted him to go to college. He had an offer to go to a college in Florida — on a *football* scholarship!

Hank attended Central High School, then finished at Josephine Allen Institute, a private school. For two years, Hank played

18

halfback and end on his high school team, one year leading Central in touchdowns, but gave up football to devote himself completely to baseball.

Neither school had a baseball team, so Hank played softball, doing "a little of everything. If they needed a pitcher, I'd go in and pitch a little bit. If they needed somebody to play first base, I'd play first base. I played just about all the positions."

On week ends, though, Hank would play hardball. He was with the recreation department league when Ed Scott, who is now a full-time scout with the Boston Red Sox, invited him to play hardball with his team, the Mobile Black Bears. A few weeks later, Hank showed up, and began playing regularly with the team, receiving a few dollars for each outing. On the last Sunday of the season, the barnstorming Indianapolis Clowns of the Negro American League played the Bears and Hank impressed the touring pros enough to be asked if he'd like to play with the Clowns. "Why sure, I'd like to give it a try," Hank said. The late Bunny Downs said he'd send Hank a contract to join the Clowns.

3

Hank Becomes a Clown

IT WASN'T until the next spring when Hank was a graduating senior that the contract for what seemed like a fantastic $200 a month arrived in the mail. Hank was elated. To him, the Negro American League was the big leagues (since Jackie Robinson had only recently broken the color barrier in the majors).

His parents didn't want him to go. His father thought he should go to college, and so did his mother. Actually, "my mother just wanted me to stay home. She didn't think I was old enough or mature enough to go any place or do anything on my own." But eighteen-year-old Henry won them over.

Imagine being paid to do something he loved so well! But "I wasn't really thinking about the living. What I wanted to do was play baseball. I felt if I could play good enough, I would definitely make a good living at it." (And he has — at $125,000 a year, he's one of baseball's highest-paid stars.)

But as he left for Winston-Salem, North Carolina, where the Clowns were in spring training, all his parents could afford to give him was a flimsy suitcase, two dollars, two sandwiches, and a pair of trousers. Hank recalls: "I swore right then that when I came back I was going to have me a pocketful of money and three pairs of black shoes." (He made good on part of that vow. When he came back that spring, he cashed a $200 check and got nothing but one-dollar bills. The 200 singles made quite a pocketful.)

In spite of Hank's eagerness to play, he was apprehensive and frightened. His parents and some of his brothers and sisters came to see him off on the train that would take him out of Mobile for the first time. They had their doubts, and he certainly had his. As Hank explains it, he really had no idea of how good he was because he had played hardball only on week ends. "I was taking a chance going there, trying to win jobs from veterans who had been with the Clowns twelve or thirteen years."

At first it seemed he wasn't going to get the chance. The day he reported "was cold, in the forties, and I didn't have a warm-up jacket and they wouldn't give me one. I didn't have a baseball to throw. I just had to pick my way."

Homesick and discouraged, Hank was tempted to give it all up, but his brother Herbert convinced him to hang in there and make good.

When Henry finally broke into the line-up, he was convinced "it's either now or never." He had to show what he could do then because he felt sure he wasn't going to get another chance. And show them he did, getting hits his first two times up and making some great fielding plays at shortstop. But despite his fine performance, his name was missing from the line-up card the next day, and for several days after that.

No one was giving much encouragement. In fact, sometimes it was quite the opposite, as when Hank, walking behind a pair of veteran players, heard one tell the other, "Soon we'll be up North and rid of those green kids like the punk behind us, and we can get down to business."

Henry swallowed hard, resigned to the feeling that no matter how he did — and he *had* performed well — he was going to be headed back to Mobile.

It was a week before he got a chance to play again. In that game in Indianapolis, Henry went four-for-four, and he stayed in the line-up after that.

Getting from one game to another was an experience in itself. Sometimes the Clowns would play as many as three games in a single day, say a double-header in Washington in the afternoon and a game in Baltimore that same night. "We'd be in Washington one day and drive to Alabama that night. The bus would break down and we'd have to wait on the side of the road. Sometimes the driver would fall asleep while driving, and we'd be half on the shoulder of the road before he woke up. We were kind of scared all night."

One time the team made a 900-mile hop, leaving Chattanooga, Tennessee, after a night game, riding all night, all the next day, and part of the next too.

There's a story that Hank (who still likes a nap the afternoon before a night game) once slept from the time he got on the bus in Washington, until the team arrived in

Buffalo, New York — twenty-four hours later.

However long he slept, he was ready for action when he got there. In the double-header in Buffalo, against the Kansas City Monarchs, Hank homered and followed with a single and two doubles, ending the day with ten hits in eleven times at bat.

"We'll be all right after we get rid of those green punk kids," Hank said, applying the needle to the player who had used almost the same words about him.

4

That's No Way
to Hold a Bat

SURPRISINGLY, Henry started out hitting cross-handed. In other words, though his left side was toward the pitcher, in the customary right-hand hitter's stance, he held his bat with his left hand above his right. This is definitely unorthodox and probably cost him ten or twenty points on his batting average, though he could hit with power that way. Hank advises against anybody following his example. However, it did have some value. "I think it had a lot to do with the development of my wrists, actually, because you really had to be quick," he said. Hank's quick, strong wrists, thicker in diameter than former heavyweight champion Floyd Patterson's, and his sinewy fore-arms are among Aaron's prime hitting assets.

The late Dewey Griggs, a scout for the Braves who would eventually sign him, was the first to try to correct Hank's batting grip. "Now I just want you to go up there and put your right hand on top of the left hand and try hitting that way," he told Hank before a Clowns' game. Henry took the suggestion, and got three hits. But even later, in the minors, when the pitcher got two strikes on him, and his manager wasn't looking, Hank would sneak his left hand back on top because he felt more sure of hit-ting the ball with a cross-handed grip.

Actually, it was a dangerous way to hit, because a fast ball inside could crack the wrist. (He had some trouble hitting inside pitches cross-handed.) What surprises Henry is that up until then neither Buster Haywood, the Clowns' manager, nor anyone else had tried to change Hank's grip, or rec-ommend that Hank become a switch-hitter. All he had to do was cross over to the other side of the plate, and his hands would have been in normal position for a left-handed hitter.

If Hank were starting out in baseball now,

he would probably try to be a switch-hitter, he said. "Then I wouldn't have had to face right-handed pitchers like Don Drysdale from the right side. Also, hitting lefty you're a step closer to first base, and you can take advantage of bunts."

Despite his cross-hand hitting style, Hank was leading the Negro American League, hitting .467 for the Clowns, and major-league clubs took close notice.

Clowns' owner Syd Pollock whetted the Braves' interest with a "P.S." he added to a letter about another player. "Incidentally," Pollock wrote the Braves' farm director, "we have a seventeen-year-old shortstop hitting fourth, with about a .400 average." The shortstop was actually eighteen-year-old Hank, who impressed Braves' scout Griggs with a seven-for-eight day, in which he smacked a low outside pitch over the right-field fence, walloped a high inside ball for a homer to left, and beat out a bunt.

The Giants made a bid for Hank, and only a matter of $200 stood in the way of Hammerin' Hank's eventually joining Wondrous Willie Mays in the Giants' outfield. The Giants wanted Hank to play with their Sioux Falls, South Dakota, Class A team, but they offered $200 less than the Braves, who wanted Hank on their Class C team at Eau Claire, Wisconsin, in the Northern League. The choice was simple, and about two-and-a-half months into the 1952 season, Henry's father signed the contract for Henry (who was legally too young to sign for himself) to enter the Braves' farm system for $350 a month.

The Clowns got $10,000 for Hank — part of it immediately and the rest to be added if and when the young ballplayer made his way up through the farm system to the major leagues. In those days, players got no bonuses for signing, so Hank didn't make a nickel on the transaction (though the Clowns' owner gave him a cardboard suitcase as a going-away present). The sale price was a lot of money then, "but nowadays it would be insulting to a player," Hank comments.

To join the team at Eau Claire, Henry had to take a plane. It was his first trip by air and Hank, who still does not feel completely at ease in the sky, rode that plane from Charlotte, North Carolina, as if it were a bronco, shaking all the way.

Once on the ground, he did fine, especially with his hot bat. In two weeks, he was named to the league's All-Star team, and in

87 games that season, Hank laced out 116 hits in 345 at-bats, for a sizzling .336 average. He batted in 61 runs, scored 79, stole 25 bases, and socked 9 homers, 4 triples, and 19 doubles. He was voted the league's Most Outstanding Rookie.

At Eau Claire, Henry played shortstop, where, he said, he had a tendency to throw the ball underhand and the ball had a tendency to sink before it got to first. Thus, most of his errors came not from missing the ball but from throwing it away.

The late Billy Southworth, then a scout for the Braves, saw enough in the young ballplayer's performance, however, to report: "Aaron has all the qualifications of a major-league shortstop."

Southworth's letter to John Quinn, then the Braves' general manager, said that Aaron, who was hitting .345 at the time, "is a line-drive hitter, although he has hit a couple of balls out of the park for home runs. He has good hands, also quick hands, gets the ball away fast and accurately. He gets a good jump on the ball and can range far to right or left. I saw him go deep in the hole to his right and field a slow-hit ball. He came up throwing and virtually shot his man out going to first. This was a big-league play in my book because I did not think he had a chance to retire the man at first. He has a strong arm. Aaron started two double-plays and completed one from the pivot position. Aaron throws a lot like Maranville, not over-handed but sidearm. His arm is strong and he does not have to straighten up to throw."

Southworth was impressed by Henry's hands and with the fact that Hank was only eighteen. He reported that Hank "runs better than average so I would have to call him fast but not very fast." Then he added, "Please don't get the impression that Aaron isn't a good runner, because he is fast and his running will continue to improve for the next couple of years."

In the second game that Southworth watched, Aaron hit a long home run over the left-center-field fence the first time, and ended the evening with three hits and three RBI's. He made one error in four chances, and stole a base.

"For a baby-faced kid of eighteen years, his playing ability is outstanding," Southworth concluded.

The next season, the Braves promoted Hank to their Class A team, the Tars, in

Jacksonville, Florida, in the South Atlantic League (usually called the Sally League).

There, he had a year that can be fairly described as "fantastic." He led the league in just about everything — batting average (.362), hits (208), RBI's (125), total bases (338), and doubles (36). His 22 home runs were "only" enough for second place in that department, but he was elected the Sally League's Most Valuable Player, getting 75 per cent of the votes cast.

Good as his year was, Hank did not play flawlessly. As a second baseman, he made more than his share of errors (according to one source, he led the league in that department). "I wasn't afraid of the runner," Hank recalls, "but I wanted to get the ball as quickly as possible and get rid of it. I made a lot of mistakes, dropped a lot of balls, couldn't make the right pivot." Once, a forced-out runner from first base failed to slide, and the ball Hank was gunning to first for the attempted double-play caught him in the ear. The incident, which Hank regrets to this day, ended the career of the runner, a good major-league prospect.

Hank was himself the victim of an opposing second baseman, when in one memorable game he managed to steal second base three times. Each time, though, he left the bag before the crafty infielder had returned the ball to the pitcher, and Hank's three steals became three outs.

Needless to say, Henry got a good chewing out from his manager, the late Ben Geraghty, who taught Hank to learn from his boners and never to make the same mistake twice. "Ben never said anything after we lost," Hank recalls, "but if we made mistakes in a game we won, we'd hear about them." It was the Jacksonville pilot who turned Hank into a student of the game. Rather than tell his rookie how good he was, he emphasized how good a player he could become.

Hank considers Geraghty "the greatest manager I ever played for, perhaps the greatest manager who ever lived, and that includes the managers in the big leagues. I've never played for a guy who could get more out of every ballplayer than he could. He knew how to communicate with everybody and to treat every player as an individual."

Hank's high opinion was based as much on Geraghty as a human being as on his baseball know-how.

The manager's sensitivity was particularly appreciated by Hank and his Jacksonville

Hank gets advice from Ben Geraghty, "the greatest manager I ever played for." As Jacksonville minor leaguer in 1953, Henry was voted Sally League's MVP.

teammates, Felix Mantilla and Horace Garner. As the first blacks to play in the Sally League, they were subject to all kinds of abuse. Fans shouted insults, people called them names and wrote threatening letters. The Jacksonville fans, Hank remembers, "were cold to us for months. They couldn't believe we were in the same ballpark that ten years earlier wouldn't let Jackie Robinson suit up." When the club was on the road, Aaron, Mantilla, and Garner had to live apart from their teammates because of discrimination: "Ben Geraghty would come over to us after every game, and maybe have dinner with us and spend hours with us talking baseball.

"I can't ever forget that because the man really went out of his way. He didn't have to do it. He could have said, 'the heck with it, play and that's it.' He was just a great manager."

Eventually, though, the fans warmed up to the newcomers. In the team's first exhibition game Hank hit one out of the park for Jacksonville's only run in a 20-1 exhibition rout by the Boston Red Sox. But when his team played other Sally League teams, Jacksonville dominated the competition. In a few weeks fans and writers were urging that

Jacksonville be taken out of the league — the team was too strong.

For something like forty-eight years, Jacksonville had never won a pennant. But in 1953, they did, led by Hank's hot bat. It was one of Hank's more satisfying accomplishments.

With the pennant nailed down, Hank got a chance to play the outfield. Since the Braves had some fine infield prospects coming along, it was felt that Hank could make it to the big leagues sooner as an outfielder.

That winter he was sent to Puerto Rico to learn to play the outfield, and manager Mickey Owen, the former Dodger catcher, had Hank hit to left field and to right field for a few hours before each game.

At this time, the Braves made a trade with the New York Giants to get Bobby Thomson. Hank learned that he was to have been part of that deal, but that the Braves wanted to hold on to him. Henry was disappointed. He felt that he might have become a Giants' outfielder.

5

Hank "Breaks" into
the Majors

WELL, Hank told himself, he *wasn't* going to the Giants. Now that the Braves had Thomson to play the outfield for them, Hank resigned himself to another year in the minors. When the Braves' spring training opened at St. Petersburg, Florida, he was ticketed for the AAA league club in Toledo, Ohio. Then Thomson broke his ankle sliding into base. Charlie Grimm, the Braves' manager, gave Hank a glove and told him to play left field.

The next day at Payne Park in Sarasota, Florida, Hank belted three hits, including what may be the longest homer he's ever hit, over a row of trailers that bordered the

Charley Grimm glad-hands Hank as he rounds third on homer in 1954 spring training. The rookie's booming bat convinced the Braves' manager that he was the man to replace the injured Bobby Thomson.

field. It proved to Grimm that Aaron could sock the long ball, and he told a jubilant Hank, "The job is yours."

So instead of spending at least another year in the minors as he had expected, twenty-year-old Henry Aaron was a major leaguer, the starting left fielder for the Milwaukee Braves.

"I think I was too young or too dumb to be scared," he says now with an infectious laugh. He felt he was going to stick as a big leaguer, though he made "a lot of mistakes" at the beginning.

He was constantly throwing to the wrong base, and made more than his share of boners as a baserunner. Hank can still remember one game in Chicago. The Braves were losing by two runs, and there was one out in a late inning when Hank singled. With slugger Eddie Mathews at the plate, he foolishly tried to steal second and was thrown out. Mathews followed with a homer that would have tied the game had Hank stayed at first.

"That was really stupid," Hank said recently, adding that many young ballplayers do this sort of thing. "But I was fortunate enough to come under a very good manager [Grimm], who didn't criticize me in front of the others, but took me aside and told me it was a very dumb play I made because even if I steal second base and Mathews gets a base hit, we're still a run behind."

Another time, with no outs and his team behind by a run, Hank tried to score from third on a short fly to left and was easily thrown out at the plate. The next man up hit a fly that was deep enough for Hank to have walked home, had he stayed at third.

Former Brave Bill Bruton recalled: "When he first joined our team, we held our breath when a fly ball was hit in his direction. It was the way he went after the ball, like he was never going to get there. But after we saw him awhile and saw the kind of things he could do, we didn't worry any more."

The fleet-footed, steady Bruton was in center field next to Hank and he helped to take some of the early pressure off while Hank was adjusting to the outfield.

"But the only way you're going to learn," according to Hank, "is to profit by your mistakes. If you go out there and make a bad play or throw to the wrong base, just make sure you don't do it again."

Hank learned his lessons well. Today he knows how to play the hitters, to the point where he not only adjusts his playing location from one batter to the next, but may even shade a few steps one way or another on the same batter as the count changes.

"It's a matter of experience plus knowing who's pitching for you, and being aware of different situations," he explains. "If I was playing behind a pitcher like [Warren] Spahn [the great Brave left-hander], and in the clubhouse meeting he had said, 'I'm going to pitch him inside, so shade him to left field because he'll pull,' you know that Spahn is not going to be off that much, and you shade him to the left. But you get a wild kid out there, and he might say he's going to pitch him inside but throw him outside, and the batter may pop it down the right-field line."

So sometimes the strategy backfires, Hank concedes, "but other times those couple of steps make it possible to make the catch."

Hank showed his greatness early, quickly turning the Braves' "ho-hums" about him into "oh-boys."

"Magic is the only way to describe it," Bobby Thomson said in a newspaper interview in the *Atlanta Constitution* in 1970. "I mean you just had this feeling — even then — that this guy was something special. He was far removed from the 'ordinary class' of ballplayer, like the rest of us.

"Some of the fellows were a little skeptical, really, when in 1954 the Braves' front office told us this young kid, Henry Aaron, would be in spring training with us. Everybody had said he was bound to be a great one, but nobody gave him much thought. He'd hit well in the minors, sure, but we figured he'd be like so many rookies before him — come to camp with the reputation, really see the curve ball for the first time, and bomb out.

"Well Henry Aaron bombed out — he started bombing base hits right away.

"I think we realized right then that we were seeing a young guy who was bound to become one of the game's biggest stars.

"Henry had the greatest hand action — the most lethal way of whipping that bat around that I've ever seen. And he hit nothing but line drives. Even on home runs, those balls jumped out like they'd been fired out of a cannon."

It wasn't long before Henry really started the bombardment.

The 1954 season opener was against the Reds at Cincinnati. Joe Nuxhall, the Reds' pitcher, held Aaron hitless in five at-bats. But the genial left-hander, now a broadcaster, wouldn't always be that lucky against Hank, who, he said, was the best hitter in the league. "He hit anything you threw up at him. Once I threw him a low inside curve — the ball was six inches inside — and he hit it half way up the light tower in *right*-center field." Nuxhall respected Hank's ability to hit to all fields (Hank is essentially a pull hitter today) and the fact that he always hit the ball with authority — his hits were solid, not scratchy.

The second day of the 1954 season, the Braves returned to Milwaukee to play the Cardinals, with Vic Raschi on the mound. "Nobody on our team seemed to know anything about Aaron," Raschi remembered, "except Eddie Stanky, the manager. He knew that Aaron was a potentially fine player, and he talked about everything — except the way Henry parted his hair."

On Hank's first at-bat in County Stadium, Milwaukee, he just about parted the ball, socking a double off the left-field wall, his first major-league hit. About eight days later, he faced Raschi again, and went three-for-seven, including his first big-league home run.

Hank's last homer of the season was also off Raschi, who recalls that the Cardinals

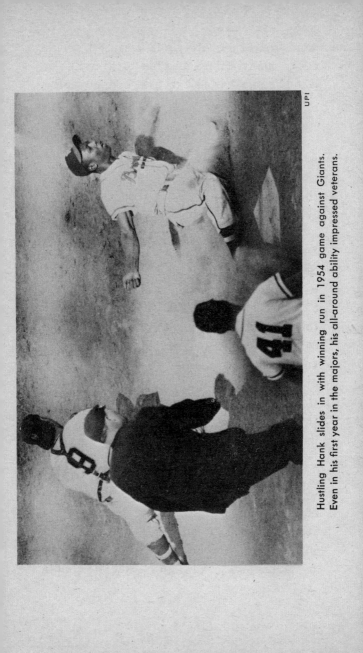

Hustling Hank slides in with winning run in 1954 game against Giants. Even in his first year in the majors, his all-around ability impressed veterans.

were impressed with Hank because he could do so many things and do them well. He could "run, steal, field, throw, and, of course, hit," said Raschi. "He had such great wrists, like Ernie Banks; it was hard to fool him."

By the season's end, Henry had 13 homers, 69 RBI's, and 131 hits for a solid .280 average, and he was runner-up to Wally Moon of the Cardinals for Rookie-of-the-Year honors.

Splendid as Hank's freshman season was, he might have done even better, had it not been for an ironic twist of fate. In an early September double-header in which he was five-for-five, the rookie Aaron, who had made it to the majors because of another player's broken ankle, suffered a similar accident himself. Like Thomson, Hank was put out of action by a slide into base. While running out a triple, Henry's powerful slide into third cracked his ankle, sidelined him for the rest of the season, and gave him a draft deferment. It also caused him to start hitting off his front foot.

"I haven't seen a hitter yet who does everything perfectly," Hank commented recently. "They say you should keep your bat still, but Ted Williams, one of the greatest hitters I've ever seen, would always twist the bat in his hand, and Stan Musial stood quite a ways from the plate. All hitters have some faults. It's what you can do to recover from these faults," said Hank. For him, it's his wrists. They have the power and quickness to more than make up for any technical defects, such as the hitch in his swing (which stops incidentally, when the pitcher gets ready to throw).

"Most players couldn't hit the way I do," he said. "I'm fortunate that all the things you have to do in baseball come naturally to me. I do have a hitch in my swing, and I hit off the front foot. I've seen the movies. The weight is forward, but you notice the hands are always back. If they throw me a change-up, I'm not out in front."

If Hank tried to model himself after any particular ballplayer it was probably Joe DiMaggio, the great Yankee center fielder, a symbol of cool perfection, who could make the most difficult plays look easy. "He threw to the right base, he could run, he hit with power," Hank says. "He was the type of player, who, to me, did everything right. This symbolizes a *great* ballplayer."

Hank doesn't remember playing against Joltin' Joe, but he did have the tremendous thrill of playing against his boyhood idol, Jackie Robinson. In one game, Hank faked bunts twice against Jackie, who made no move to field them. Jackie is reported to have said, "We'd rather have you bunting in this ballpark than swinging away. Anytime you want to bunt we'll give you first base, just so you don't get anything more."

Jackie's former Dodger teammate, Pee Wee Reese, was impressed from the beginning with the way Hank swung and used his quick hands. "That's a heck of a ballplayer, we thought," said Reese. Pee Wee, who played against Hank in the 1950's, never saw Aaron throw to the wrong base or make a bad play. "He had a good arm. He was never flashy in the field, but he always got there. Hank is right up with the Mayses, Musials, Mantles, Williamses, and DiMaggios."

Any doubts that his freshman showing was "a flash in the pan" were wiped out in the following season when Hank whacked the ball at a .314 clip (to tie for fifth place in the league) while swatting 27 homers and knocking in 106 runs, one more than he scored. He led the league in doubles with 37, an honor he'd win at least three more times.

The Braves, who had finished in third place in 1954, eight games behind the pennant-winning Giants, moved up to second in

1955, but were 13½ games out. Still they knew they were developing into a good ball club.

Henry was developing not only as a ball-player, but as a dry humorist. During the season, when light-hitting Danny O'Connell was injured, Hank replaced him at second base for twenty-seven games. When hard-hitting Henry received his contract for the next season, he quipped, "I think you sent me Danny O'Connell's by mistake."

(Hank, who started out in major-league ball at $5,000 a year; moved to the $100,000 club in 1967; signed a two-year contract for $250,000 before the 1970 season, and reportedly signed a three-year $600,000 contract; has had no serious pay disputes.)

During these early games especially, Hank studied the pitchers. As he got to know them better, he developed more confidence in his ability to hit, and predicted before the 1956 season that he'd raise his average fifteen points. Actually he raised it fourteen, and his .328 mark led the league that year. He beat out such solid hitters as Bill Virdon, Roberto Clemente, and Stan Musial to do it. Coupled with the batting crown, Henry led both leagues with 200 base hits, which included 26 homers, 14 triples, and 34 league-leading doubles, for 340 total bases — tops in the league. These were remarkable achievements for any ballplayer, especially for a twenty-two-year-old in just his third year in the majors.

Don Davidson, the Braves' traveling secretary, first suggested Hammerin' Hank as a nickname for Henry, and it was a natural.

Hank's 1956 slugging percentage — total bases divided by times at bat — was high enough for him to tie for third, and his twenty-five-game hitting streak was the longest of the season.

About a quarter of the way through the 1956 season, Charlie Grimm was replaced as the Braves' manager by Fred Haney, one of the strictest men Hank ever played for. To Hank's way of thinking, Haney inherited a great ball club, and few would disagree. Among the players were the pitching greats, Warren Spahn and Lew Burdette, and the slugging third baseman, Eddie Mathews (who later rejoined the Braves as batting coach and became manager in 1972).

One day Hank hit a sharp grounder against Ruben Gomez of the Giants and thought he ran it out. But Haney chewed him out over it. What got the usually unrufflable Aaron upset was that the manager had done it in front of the rest of the club. Always a proud man, Henry resented being embarrassed that way and told the manager, "If you want to scold me, do it in private." They never had problems after that.

"Of all the managers I've played for [he's had eight major-league pilots] I've had no trouble with any of them. I think anytime you see friction on a ball club between players and a manager, it's usually 'fringe' ballplayers, players who are looking for an excuse and somebody to blame. They'll say things like, 'The reason I didn't have a good season is he didn't pitch me every four days, or he didn't let me play regularly.' "

From a mediocre 24-22 record, the Braves got hot and were soon feeling symptoms of pennant fever. They went down to the wire but were edged out on the last day of the season. It was a bitter antifever pill to swallow, but there was always next year.

6

1957 Was a Very Good Year

HANK shot off to a great season that next year — 1957. The Braves stayed neck-and-neck for first place with the Cardinals. On June 28 Hank tripled home a pair of runs to give the Braves a 2-1 victory over the Dodgers and keep his club in the thick of the race a half game behind the Cards. Two days later, his three-run homer broke a 6-6 tie with the Pirates, leading the Braves to a 13-6 win — and first place.

He was devastating, no matter what kind of pitching he faced. In early July he was hitting better than .350 and also leading in RBI's and homers. Hank seemed headed for the Triple Crown (tops in RBI's, homers, and batting average). Then in Philadelphia he tripped on a soda bottle a fan had thrown, and twisted his ankle. This sidelined him for a week, and when he came back into the line-up, perhaps too soon, he developed some bad habits that would cost him the batting title.

More important, there was a pennant at stake. Five clubs were bunched within two or three games of one another for first place in the National League (there were no divisions then). Then, in early August, the Braves launched a ten-game win streak. On September 3 they led the Cardinals by 8½ games, and it seemed like easy sailing, but the lead ebbed away, and by September 15, the margin was a slim 2½ games. Once again the Braves rebounded, winning game after game.

On September 22 Hank hit his forty-second four-bagger of the season, tying him for the lead with Ernie Banks, and the Braves beat the Cubs in ten innings 9-7. They needed just one more victory to clinch the National League pennant.

It would be especially sweet to nail it down at home, where they were playing the Cardinals the following night. At Milwaukee, where attendance records were being broken, a partisan crowd of 40,926 turned out for what they hoped would be the clincher, but the Cardinals weren't going to roll over and play dead. At the end of nine innings, the score was tied at two all. It stayed that way through the tenth and the top of the eleventh.

In the home half of the eleventh, Johnny Logan singled for the Braves and the potential pennant-winning run was on base. Slugger Eddie Mathews flied out. Two outs, and now it was up to clean-up hitter Hank Aaron, the man who'd sparked the Braves to first place. He'd had two hits already, one of which contributed to a run in the second inning. The fans yelled for Hank to hit one out of the park, but on the mound was Billy Muffett (now a pitching coach), who hadn't thrown a gopher ball in ages.

Muffett wound up and threw a curve; Hank lashed out, connected, and drove the ball to dead center. At the 402-foot sign, Wally Moon made a desperation leap but came down empty-handed. The ball was gone, Hank had his forty-third home run, and the Braves had a 4-2 win and the National League pennant!

The crowd went wild. Hank was mobbed by his teammates and carried on their shoulders into the dugout. The *Milwaukee Journal*

Victorious Braves carry Hank from field after he nails down 1957 National League pennant with eleventh-inning homer. The Braves went on to win the World Series and Hank was voted the National League's MVP.

joyfully quoted from the Bible, "For Aaron stretched out his hand with his rod and smote the dust of the earth." Then it added: "Verily he did, and at 11:34 last night, he also smote a baseball over the center-field fence at County Stadium. The grand result of this was that Milwaukee clinched its first National League pennant since the Braves arrived here five delirious seasons ago."

"When Hank hit that pitch, I knew it was a homer," said Lou Perini, who was then the Braves' owner. "But it was the slowest homer I ever saw in my life. I thought it would never get over the fence."

For Hank, hitting the homer — an "important one" like Thomson's — was probably the most exciting moment in his baseball career. "I wasn't really thinking about hitting a home run, but I had had a great season and so this kind of climaxed it all," he said.

The celebrations lasted into the early hours of the morning, and Hank expected he'd be given the next game off. But he was in the line-up. He wasn't sorry; he socked a pitch from Sam Jones for a grand-slam homer, the first of his career (he now has thirteen grand slams, more than any other active player). It was his forty-fourth home run of the season, enough to give him the season's title in that category. He also led the league in runs batted in (132), runs scored (118), and total bases (369).

Despite a very respectable .322 average, he was beaten out for the batting title, finishing in a tie for third. Had he won in that category, he would have earned the Triple Crown. Several times in later seasons he'd win two of the categories, but miss out on the third. There hasn't been a National League Triple Crown winner in years (in the American League, Frank Robinson did it in 1966 and Carl Yastrzemski did it in 1967), and Hank would very much like to turn the trick.

If he needed consolation — who would with that record? — he got it, but good. Hank was elected the league's Most Valuable Player, edging out Musial for the honor, by a 239-230 vote among the twenty-four members of the Baseball Writers Association (three from each National League city). Hank was named on every ballot.

It was a time for rejoicing. What would make it even more of a jubilee would be a World Series victory. That was a tall order, for the Braves' opponent would be the New York Yankees, who had clinched the American flag the same day the Braves did the National. Pennant winners eight of the past nine years, the Yankees had a roster of Series veterans, while, except for Warren Spahn, Red Schoendienst, and Andy Pafko, it was the first time any of the Braves had been in a Series.

Milwaukee gave the Braves a rousing send-off, even excusing some schoolchildren from class to participate. On Monday, the day before the opener, the Braves worked out at Yankee Stadium, whose perilous left-field shadows they'd heard so much about and which would be primarily Wes Covington's problem; Hank was in center field.

The Yankees, being World Champions, were naturally favored to win. As far as most newspapermen were concerned, Hank recalled, between the shadows and the pressure, the Braves were defeated before they started.

"The opening day crowd (69,476) didn't scare us — we were used to big crowds in Milwaukee — but just the idea of playing in the World Series, and millions of people all over the United States watching us on TV, just scared me to death," Hank said. He knew back home they were intently watching the first Mobile boy to make it this far in baseball.

Whitey Ford pitched the opener for the Bronx Bombers, and had tense Hank swinging at some bad curve balls. Aaron managed a single in the fourth, but in the sixth, with New York ahead 1-0 and two men on, he struck out on three straight curves. The last, which Aaron protested, was supposed to have been a waste pitch; Hank was unable to check his swing.

His teammates didn't do any better against the sharp twirler, who allowed only five hits, and the Yankees had a tidy 3-1 opening-game victory.

The Braves felt badly enough about the loss; they felt worse about the razzing that a couple of the Yankees gave them, calling them "bush." A meeting was called before the second game, and the Milwaukee players comforted each other, saying, "We're in the World Series, but it's just another baseball game. We've got to feel we've got the best ball club out there. Now let's go out and play our game."

Play they did. Wes Covington made a great catch; Lew Burdette held the Yankees to two runs while the Braves batted across four. Hank scored one of the runs in the second inning after he blasted a towering drive to center that Mickey Mantle played badly. Mickey was playing deep on Aaron (the man Mantle considers "the best ballplayer of my era"). But he wasn't deep enough and though he lunged desperately, the ball got by him for a triple. Hank then scored on Joe Adcock's single.

The Series, tied at a game apiece, now moved to Milwaukee. Bob Buhl would pitch for the Braves against Bob (No Wind-Up) Turley. In the Yankee first, Tony Kubek homered with one out, Mantle and Yogi Berra walked. Buhl wheeled and tried to pick Mantle off second, but threw into center field. Though Red Schoendienst sort of sat on him, Mickey made it to third base and Yogi to second. Gil McDougald hit a high fly to center and Aaron raced for it; stumbling, he slid to his knees and caught the sinking ball in the webbing of his glove, which was flat on the ground. The umpire ruled it an out, but a fan's photographs indicated the ball was on the ground. "Pictures can be deceiving," Hank says. "The umpire made the right call because I definitely did catch the ball."

As it turned out, it hardly mattered. Mantle scored after the catch, a single drove in

Berra, the Yanks were ahead 3-0, and would end on top of a 12-3 rout.

In the fifth, Hank, oh-for-two, faced Don Larsen, who had pitched the perfect World Series game the year before and had retired seven men in a row this game, bringing his streak to thirty-four. Logan singled to end the streak. After Larsen got Mathews on a fly, he went behind on Aaron. Expecting Larsen to come in with a pitch, Hank set himself and drove the ball over the barrier in right center. (Larsen said afterward, "It was a bad pitch, not a strike — a fast ball, high and outside.") The blow brought the Braves within four, but the game was a lost cause.

One of the stories told again and again about Hank involves Yogi Berra, the Yankee catcher, who liked to talk to hitters to get their minds off what they were up there to do. (Now a Mets' coach, he still likes to talk.)

In the Series, so the story goes, Yogi told Hank, "Hey, kid, you're holding your bat wrong. It's supposed to be with the label up." And Hank replied, "I didn't come here to read," and promptly walloped a base hit.

It's a good story. The trouble is, like so many others told about Henry, it just isn't true. It may be that stories like these are made up to make Henry into the "colorful character" that he's the first one to admit he isn't. He's warm, sincere, and the sort of person people enjoy meeting, but he just doesn't chatter or dress flamboyantly, kick at the water cooler or lose his hat. Low key has been the style of this quiet professional who had come to the World Series to hit.

Warren Spahn took the mound for the Braves in the fourth game, and gave up a run in the first. In the fourth, after Logan had singled and Mathews, hitless in nine at-bats, had doubled, the Yankees let Tom Sturdivant pitch to Henry, who had slammed a sharp grounder into the hole and beaten it out in the second inning. This time, with the count one and one, he drove a shot deep to left for a three-run homer. (It was his second four-bagger of the series and the sixth hit.) Frank Torre also homered that inning to give the Braves a three-run lead that held up until the ninth when Elston Howard belted a three-run equalizer.

In the top of the tenth, Hank Bauer drove in the go-ahead run for the Yankees with a triple. In the Braves' half, pinch-hitter Nippy Jones showed there was shoe polish on the ball* to prove to the plate umpire the

---

* Another Jones — Cleon — used the same polish proof to get on base for the New York Mets in the 1969 Series.

pitch had hit him, and was awarded the base. Felix Mantilla, who ran for him, was sacrificed to second, and scored the tying run on Logan's double. Mathews won it for the Braves 7-5 with a towering right-field homer. The Series was tied again.

Game number five was a duel of pitchers Burdette and Ford. Coming into the sixth, neither had given up a run. With two outs, Mathews grounded to second base. Jerry Coleman waited for a good hop, enough of a lapse to let Mathews beat it out. On an inside pitch, Aaron hit a high fly that dropped in between Bauer and Coleman in short right, and then Adcock singled Mathews in for the game's only run. Hank was now eight for nineteen, a whopping .421 average, and the Braves had a 3-2 Series lead.

In the sixth game, back at Yankee Stadium, Wes Covington continued his sparkling outfield play, throwing Berra out at the plate, an act he couldn't repeat when Yogi drove one out of the park for two runs. Torre, who'd hit only five home runs all season, brought the Braves within a run of the Yankees when he hit his second of the Series. Then in the top of the seventh, Hank Aaron caught hold of a Bob Turley fast ball and clouted a tremendous drive over the fence and into the left-field bullpen to tie the game. The Yankees' Hank (Bauer) put New York ahead again in the bottom of the same stanza, with a homer that caromed off the left-field foul screen. The Braves got the tying run on in the ninth in the person of Eddie Mathews, and it was up to Aaron. But Henry was caught looking on a low sinker. The Yankees won the game 3-2, and the Series was tied at three all.

Spahn was due to pitch the tie-breaker for Milwaukee, but he had the flu, so Burdette, who had already won two games in the Series, would be on the mound, trying for the Herculean goal that only six hurlers before him had attained: three victories in a single Series. Larsen would go for New York.

In the third inning, after a man was out, Bob Hazle singled for the Braves. Kubek, who had played third base, left field, and center for the Yankees, was now holding down the hot corner. He handled a grounder off Logan's bat, but his throw pulled Coleman off the bag at second, and all hands were safe. Mathews then doubled both men home. Aaron greeted Bobby Shantz, who had relieved Larsen, by punching a single to center, scoring Mathews. Covington singled Henry to third and he streaked home on a fielder's choice. Burdette held New York in check, the Braves won 5-0, and Milwaukee had its first World Championship.

When the final out was registered, strangers in the Braves' hometown hugged each other and danced in the streets, women wept, horns tooted, factory whistles blew. Mayor Frank Zeidler and his aides rushed to the bell tower and took turns clanging the bell. There were snake dances in the streets, and a crowd estimated at 400,000 hailed the conquering heroes on a victory ride five miles through the city.

Hank Aaron had had quite a Series, leading both clubs in batting average (.393) and RBI's (7), and by getting at least one hit in every game. In 28 times at bat, he had 11 hits, including 3 homers and a triple; and scored 5 runs. It was a rousing climax to a remarkable year.

7

Thrilling, Even to
an Old Pro

HANK AARON knows from past experience
what a thrill it is to be in a World Series.
That's why, once the Braves were eliminated
in 1970, he rooted for the Cubs to win so
Ernie Banks might enjoy that experience.

"The player who's never been in one
doesn't know what a thrill you get. It's not
so much the money — the money's good —
but just the thrill of walking down the street,
and hearing the kids and the grownups say,
'There goes Henry Aaron,' 'There goes Tommie Agee' or anybody, who won the pennant,
who's world champion. Just being mentioned as world champion of baseball means
a lot.

"You've got to experience it before you can

appreciate it. If a young kid coming into the league gets satisfied too easily, he'll never appreciate it. You've always got to feel you can go up just a little bit higher."

Hank feels the same way about All-Star games as he does about the World Series. "It's a thrill to be in an all-star game, whether you're in the Little League or Pony League, no matter where it is. To be chosen to play in an all-star game is one of the greatest thrills in the world," and his enthusiasm hasn't dimmed after having played in nineteen of the interleague classics.

Hank, who got more fans' votes than any other National League player for the 1970 squad, has been named to All-Star rosters every conceivable way — by vote of fans, sportswriters, players, and managers. One year, he and Willie Mays were named by the Commissioner of Baseball to be starters, though they weren't leading the balloting for their positions. The Commissioner did this after Cincinnati fans had "packed" the voting so every starter except the pitcher (who was not elected by the fans) was a Cincy player.

Strangely, Hank's record in All-Star competition has been below par, and he comments, "If there's anything I've been discouraged with since I've been in baseball, it's my performance in All-Star games." His first All-Star extra-base hit was a homer, in 1971, and he repeated the feat in 1972. His All-Star batting average was .194, however.

And yet he has had some shining moments. For instance, his first All-Star Game in 1955: Hank entered the game as a pinch-runner, went two-for-two, and drove in the tying run to set the scene for Musial's game-winning homer in the twelfth inning.

It may be that, since hitters get perhaps only one at-bat against each of the unfamiliar pitchers for the opposing league, there's not enough time to get "on" to their stuff. Hank merely says, "I don't know what it is; I've been really lousy in All-Star competition."

Still he would be very disappointed if he weren't picked. He explains his feelings this way: "A lot of players can play a lifetime and never get picked to be on an All-Star team. They can be in the big leagues and never get a chance to *go* to an All-Star Game. So I feel it's an honor for any player, no matter who you are, to be picked to play in an All-Star Game, and you should be very, very grateful to the fans or people who choose you. And you should try to do everything you can to live up to the award they gave you."

8

Hank Does It Again

AT THE START of the 1958 season, the Braves and Hank were at the top of the world. The question was, Could they repeat their sparkling showing of the previous year?

If there were some early-season doubts, it was understandable. Hank, bothered by an abscessed tooth, was hitting below par. His average seemed anchored around the .270 level. But he broke out of his slump with five hits in six at-bats, and his average rose to .289 by All-Star time. From that point, it was onward and upward for Hank and his ball club.

In the third week of September, the

Braves were leading the Pirates by five games, and needed just one win to clinch the pennant the second year in a row.

Years before, when the Braves had two fine starters on their staff — Johnny Sain and Warren Spahn — and little more pitching strength, the joke used to be that the Braves starting pitching rotation was "Spahn and Sain, and pray for rain."

Sain was gone, but Spahn was still performing brilliantly. He was on the mound in the try for the clincher, against the Reds in Cincinnati. It was a scoreless tie into the fifth inning, when Spahn took matters into his own batting hands. He led off with a double and scored on singles by Bill Bruton, and Red Schoendienst, the veteran the Braves had acquired midway through the 1957 season and the man many said was the key to the 1957 pennant. After Mathews hit into a force-out, Hank spanked a double, chasing two runs home, and, when the relay from the outfield went wild, he scored to make it 4-0.

Surprisingly, some unknowing observers have said Hank "dogs it" on the basepaths, especially down the first-base line. Hank comments: "I know they think I don't care. I look like I'm running easy to first, but I'm

Hank knows when to "shift gears" and put on speed on base paths. Here he legs out a bunt in 1955 as throw sails past Giants' first baseman, Harris.

watching the outfielder and if he messes up, I can accelerate. I have the speed to shift gears."

In the seventh inning, the Schoendienst-Aaron combination clicked again, Hank following Red's single with his thirtieth homer of the season, to give the Braves a 6-0 lead. As it turned out, the homer was the winning run, because the Reds rallied in the bottom of the inning for five runs. The 6-5 lead held up, and the Braves had another pennant.

For Henry Aaron, it was another fine year, despite the early-season slump, and he finished close to the top in batting (.326), RBI's (95), and homers (30).

So history had repeated itself — the Braves had clinched another pennant, with Hank again supplying another four-bagger. The question now was, Would Milwaukee lightning strike the Yankees again?

Whitey Ford and Warren Spahn were rematched in the first game, played at Milwaukee. Moose Skowron homered to give New York a 1-0 lead in the fourth. In the bottom of the inning, Hank drew a walk. After two infield outs, the Braves, starting to swing at Ford's first pitch, put together three singles and went ahead 2-1. But the lead lasted only into the top of the next inning, when after

Ford walked, the Yank's Hank Bauer socked a hanging screwball for a homer and a 3-2 lead.

The Braves got the tying run on first when Mathews strolled. Aaron clouted one to the right-field rail. Bauer at first thought it was headed for the seats, and decided that his only chance to catch it or stop it was to make a desperation leap. Somehow — it might have been a tricky wind — the ball went past his wrist. Aaron had a double, sending Mathews to third and Ford to the showers. After reliever Ryne Duren fanned Adcock, Mathews scored on Covington's deep out to left-center. The Braves won it in the tenth on three singles, the last by Bruton.

So Milwaukee had drawn first blood, and after the second game, the Yankees were in need of a tourniquet. In that game, the Braves scored seven runs in the first inning, leading off with Bruton's solo homer and ending with Burdette's three-run drive into the stands. For the Yankees, Bauer hit one and Mantle smote two, but the Braves took it 13-5. Aaron had two singles, one of them contributing to a run.

When the Series moved to New York, the Bombers seemed to gain strength. Larsen and Duren teamed to blank the Braves on six hits and Bauer knocked in all four New York runs with a home run and broken-bat single. Aaron went hitless in three official trips and walked once. When he was on first and Schoendienst on second, Covington hit a one-hopper that handcuffed Skowron and skipped away. The third-base coach waved Red home, but Skowron retrieved the ball and fired to the plate. Schoendienst, retreating to third, found a surprise there: Hank Aaron. In the rundown, Red was tagged out and Hank made it back to second.

The Braves regained their touch in game number four, as Spahn spun a two-hit shutout, and his teammates capitalized on New York fielding lapses to win 3-0. One of the Yankee hits was a mighty 425-foot triple by Mantle. But that was about it. Aaron, playing center and right, went two-for-four.

Leading the Series three games to one, the Braves were confident of wrapping it up in game five. In the sixth inning, with Bruton on first, Schoendienst lined a drive to left. Off at the crack of the bat, Elston Howard ran into the deadly glare, dived to his knees, stuck out his gloved hand, and made the catch. He then doubled Bruton off. It broke the Braves' back and was probably the turning point of the Series. Milwaukee got some revenge when Howard was robbed of a hit by Hank Aaron's excellent racing catch of his powerful drive, but there were no other bright spots. The Yankees, routing Burdette with a six-run rally in the sixth, won 7-0.

Despite the loss, the Braves still led in the Series, and were in high spirits. Hank even amused his teammates with an impromptu postgame imitation of Covington staggering under a fly ball he lost (the Yankee alternate left fielder, Norm Siebern, had lost one the day before).

Back in Milwaukee, Spahn was on the mound after only two days' rest in an attempt to put the Series on ice. Once again, Elston Howard was the villain. In the second, the Braves had the bases loaded, but Elston caught Logan's short fly and threw out Andy Pafko at home. In the tenth, Howard singled and scored what proved to be the winning run in the 4-3 Yankee triumph. Aaron continued his hitting ways, with three-for-five and two RBI's, but there was no joy in the Braves' dressing room. The Series was tied at three all.

So for the second year in a row, it was down to the wire, and you could cut the tension with a Louisville slugger. Del Crandall tied the final game with a homer in the sixth, but left three teammates stranded later on. Breaking the tie with a single was none other than Elston Howard, and the Yankees went on to win the game 6-2 and the World Series, four games to three. It was the first time since 1925 that a team had won the Series after having lost three of the first four games.

For Aaron, there was real satisfaction in his continuation of his fine Series performance. This year he had hit .333, getting nine hits, including two doubles, in twenty-seven times at bat. He had knocked in two runs and scored three. In the fourteen World Series games in which he played in two years, he had a .364 batting average, the third highest in history among players with more than fifty Series at-bats.

9

The Fooler

HANK AARON fools people with his easy style. Because he is graceful, sure, and invariably in the right position, he seldom is seen racing madly for a drive. As a result, some fans have the mistaken notion that he doesn't hustle.

Hank himself is aware of this. "A lot of people who'd never seen me play would come to the ballpark and would say, 'He's loafing, he's lazy.' But I *know* how to play the outfield," said Hank, who's opposed to "false" hustle.

"I had a chance to watch Joe DiMaggio play the outfield; he always played the hitters. He never was out of position. If he knew a player was going to pull the ball, he'd be over in left-center waiting for it. This is what I believe in. If I know how to play the hitters, there's no use wasting steps if I can always be there. There's no use my running after a foul ball that's twenty rows back in the stands so they can say, 'There goes Charley Hustle.' "

Braves' rooters like to recall the game when the player who is called "Charley Hustle" — Cincinnati's head-first sliding, dashing outfielder Pete Rose — raced after a foul fly down the right-field line, overshot it and ended up falling into the stands. The next day — some Brave enthusiasts say it was the very next inning — a similar pop foul was hit, and Hank Aaron nonchalantly sauntered over and caught it. They tell the story not as a put-down of Rose, but to emphasize Aaron's easy efficiency.

Rose himself declares he's never seen Aaron *not* hustle. "Sometimes people compare him with a guy like me," Rose said, "but guys have their own style, their own way of moving. Hustle doesn't mean you run all the time."

As Rose and other Reds can testify, there are games that Aaron wins without getting a hit. There was the game in which Cincy starter, John Tsitouris, led off with a walk. After Rose struck out, Alex Johnson looped a fly ball to right. Hank, racing in, realized he couldn't catch it, but pretended he could, and Tsitouris headed back toward first. Hank fielded the ball on one bounce and forced the Cincy hurler out at second. The next batter singled, but it did no harm since there was no runner beyond first.

According to Hank, that sort of deception can be pulled only on certain players. "You can do it on a pitcher, but certainly not on a fellow who plays every day. They know from the way it's hit whether you're going to be able to catch it or not. I've forced pitchers out at second several times. That's simply because they don't play every day."

Taught to catch with two hands, Hank will make one-hand stabs only when necessary, usually "when you're running and reaching" for the ball.

His most unusual catch was a one-hander in old Sportsman's Park in St. Louis. It was the second game of a double-header, a time of day when the sun comes down between the stands and there's no way to defend against it. "You put your glasses down and hope if it's hit in your direction into the sun, it will come out of it. I remember some-

Hank's casual style usually makes playing the outfield look easy. But when he has to, he will race top speed to haul in a drive at the fence or off his shoetops.

body hitting a line drive to right. I couldn't see the ball. I just stuck out my glove and it landed right in the middle. I was trying to get out of the way really."

His most unusual *miss* resulted in his giving up a "homer." He raced after a ball hit deeper by Cincinnati's Pat Corrales than he had thought it was going. It hit his glove and bounced up, and when Henry swiped at it again, the ball bounced right over the rail to give the Reds a 2-0 lead in a game they won 3-1. Hank, who surprisingly was booed, felt worse for Braves' pitcher George Stone than he did for himself.

In an average year, Hank makes only six or seven errors. "They say the biggest danger of making an error on a liner is when the ball hits right in the middle of the glove," he said. One that got away in the 1970 season did just that as Hank grabbed for it one-handed. "It seemed to me like it had a sponge and bounced right out."

Though less powerful now, since as Aaron says, "A lot of baseball's been thrown from it," Hank's arm has always been good. "It wasn't as strong as, say, Clemente's or Mays', but I had an accurate arm. I threw the ball into the infield where the infielders could handle it. I never threw over the infielder's head. All of my balls were thrown very low."

The toughest play for an outfielder to make, according to Henry, is that hit right down the line with a man on base, when the fielder has to make a split-second decision on where to throw. "Say you've got a guy like Ed Kranepool of the Mets up, and Bud Harrelson on first. On Kranepool's hit, you know you've got almost a cinch to get him at second, but if you throw there, you know Harrelson's going to score. So you have to throw to home plate."

Once the Giants were up in the ninth and Willie Mays (whom Hank calls "one of the greatest baserunners ever") was on first. When a San Francisco teammate followed with a hit down the right-field line, Hank knew he couldn't throw to second, because "all Willie needs is two steps and he's gone." Hank didn't think twice. He gunned the ball home, and Willie held at third.

For three seasons, Hank won the Gold Glove Award, given by *The Sporting News*, as the League's best defensive right fielder.

Looking back now, Hank says, "I prefer being an outfielder. An outfielder can play much longer than an infielder, especially the kind of infielder I was. I wasn't one who could get out of the way of spikes the way some of these second basemen could."

Another advantage, according to Hank, is that an outfielder has more time to concentrate on his hitting — to think about his batting mistakes — not that hitting should be, say, 90 percent of a player's game. "I think you've got to do so many other things on the baseball field to make a contribution to your club."

When Hank started his career, the type of ball club the Braves had was such that all he had to do was hit. Hank also liked to use his legs, and when Birdie Tebbetts became manager of the club late in 1961, he called a clubhouse meeting. To Hank, he said: "You like to run the bases, you like to steal, don't you?"

Hank said, "Yes."

"Well," said Tebbetts, "you can steal as many bases as you want. But don't get thrown out, because if you do, it's going to cost you $25."

"Don't worry about me paying $25," Hank reassured Tebbetts. "I just won't run." But Hank wasn't really serious — during the 1962 season, he stole a total of 15 bases.

It was under Bobby Bragan, who became manager of the Braves before the start of the 1963 season, that Hank feels he became "a complete ballplayer." It happened, he said, because Bragan wanted him to do "all the things a complete ballplayer could, like running bases and bunting. He told me, 'I want you to run, steal a little bit, become more aggressive.' " Hank, who never wanted to be a player who was *only* a hitter, welcomed the idea. In nine seasons in the majors, he'd stolen a total of 72 bases. Now, during the 1963 season alone, he stole 31. Said Bragan, "If you need a base, he'll steal it — quietly. If you need a shoestring catch, he'll make it, and his hat won't fly off and he won't fall on his butt, he does it like Di-Maggio."

Nowadays, he steals when it's important, (the decision whether to go is usually left to him) and seldom gets thrown out. In 1970, for example, a season when a plate collision caused him a painful leg injury, he stole safely nine times in nine tries. He credits his recent success ratio to the element of surprise. ("They figure, well, he can't run, he's not going"), and notes that the secret of stealing a base is "you don't steal on the catcher, you steal on the pitcher." And Hank knows how just about every pitcher in the league operates.

To Hank Aaron, baseball is basically a guessing game. "You're out there trying to outguess the pitcher and the catcher, and if you get your pitch, you hit it. That's true of good hitters. Hitters who aren't good are those who guess a pitch but foul it off or miss it entirely."

Obviously, Hank is a good guesser. At the end of the 1972 season he had 3,391 career base knocks and 6,172 total bases, a prodigious output.

Hank tries to know exactly what a pitcher's got, exactly what he's throwing, and what he'll try to do in a given situation. ("Though, with a pitcher like Gibson or Seaver, sometimes you can guess and they'll still get you out.")

Someone once wrote that Hank would deliberately swing wildly on a pitch, to entice the hurler to throw it again later at a more decisive part of the game. The slugger denies this. "Sometimes, I might look bad on a certain pitch, say a good curve ball," he says. "Well I just hate to look bad on it again. I'll be looking for it and if you throw it again, I'll be ready. I hate to look bad on the same pitch twice."

What makes the Hammer angry is the rare instance when a pitcher *consistently* throws him the same pitch in a game and succeeds in getting him out with it.

Not one to sulk, Hank declares, "If I'm moody, nobody ever knows, not even my family. If anything, I get angry with myself. Nobody else ever knows it. I never carry the game home; I never carry it to my teammates." Clete Boyer, ex-Braves' third baseman whose locker adjoined Aaron's, once commented that whether Hank has hit a pair of homers or has gone oh-for-four "he still acts the same way."

Hank believes that the account "kind of evens out" between a good pitcher and a good hitter. "A good hitter's going to get his hits, and a good pitcher's going to get you out. I've faced pitchers like Tom Seaver and Bob Gibson and gone oh-for-four and I don't feel bad. I can go home and sleep. I say, 'Well, I've done my best, because that probably is his night.' And if I go up there and hit a home run off Gibson or Seaver, I say, 'Well, I hit his mistake.' "

Aaron was always Seaver's idol, and the Mets' ace dedicated his biography to "every athlete who has been inspired by a Henry Aaron, by a champion."

"Henry was always first with me," Seaver says. "I don't find it strange at all that a white boy who wanted to become a major-league pitcher identified with a black hitter. I thought of Aaron as excellence. He was so much fun to sit and watch because he was consistent, dedicated, and yet capable of making the game look so easy to play."

Heading the list of toughest pitchers Hank has faced in his career is Curt Simmons, a left-hander who started with the Phillies and went on to the Cardinals and the Cubs. Simmons has said, "Henry Aaron is the only ballplayer I have ever seen who goes to sleep at the plate and wakes up only to swing as a pitch comes in."

The Dodgers' Don Newcombe, Don Drysdale, and Sandy Koufax — the latter two have been credited with labeling Hank "Bad Henry" — are high on the Aaron list of tough hurlers. Among pitchers still active, Hank rates Gibson and Seaver, one and two, "because they always have the same type of good stuff, and they're going to make you hit it. They're not going to lay any mediocre fast ball down the middle for you to hit. It's going to have something on it. Or they'll throw a good curve ball, not one that hangs. They're going to make the good pitches on you consistently. These are the pitchers that win.

"Juan Marichal is another one. He has such a variety of pitches. He may throw you a screwball on the outside of the plate, a slider on the inside, a fast ball on the inside. He has perhaps the most pitches of any pitcher I've seen in the big leagues, and he can control them."

Of course, Hank also has his "cousins," pitchers "I handle pretty well. They're pitchers I feel confident I'm going to get some hits off." He's too much of a gentleman to single them out.

Hank, who has played many positions (and was on the mound in 1970 for the Braves' father-son game), said he never wanted to be a pitcher. "I think I would be afraid to get out there and have great hitters like Richie Allen, Joe Torre, Rico Carty, hitting balls through the middle. I don't think my reflexes are quick enough to get out of the way," he said with a laugh.

As a pitcher, Aaron would have one advantage over every other hurler: he wouldn't have to face himself.

10

No Such Thing
as a Bad Ball

PITCHING Hank outside the strike zone doesn't guarantee immunity from the Hammer's power. Hank's zone, a manager said, is "roughly from the peak of his cap to the tops of his shoes." An exaggeration, but Aaron often swings at so-called bad balls, and has hit a lot of home runs on pitches outside the official strike zone.

Late in 1970, for example, he beat the Mets with a ninth-inning, two-run four-bagger on a pitch from Gary Gentry that was high and inside. The Braves, rallying back from being behind 7-1, had narrowed the score to 7-6. Gil Garrido was on second, one man was out, as Hank lumbered to the plate.

It was the kind of challenge Hank enjoys. With Orlando Cepeda and Rico Carty due up next, the winning run in the person of Bad Henry would not be walked.

Hank, who had almost been excused from the game when things looked hopeless, took a fast ball for a strike and fouled off the next. Two pitches missed low and outside. (Gentry contended that close ones to Hank are called balls because of his reputation. Umpires know he knows the strike zone.) A change-up outside brought the count to 3-2. Hank fouled off the next two, but connected on the third — a high inside pitch that few hitters can handle — and drove it well over the left-field fence to give the Braves the lead they didn't relinquish.

One reason Hank swings at balls outside the strike zone is that "sometimes you know what the pitcher has in mind, what pitch he wants you to hit. If he's consistently throwing you nothing but fast balls, you're going to look for a fast ball, and if you get it up high, you just want to get around on it." In the confrontation with Gentry, Hank believes a change-up would have struck him out.

Sometimes Hank may hit a pitch close to his power zone that the hurler intended to waste, but he points out that, when really good pitchers (such as Drysdale, Koufax, Gibson, Marichal, Seaver, and Ferguson Jenkins) get an 0-2 count on a hitter, "they're either going to brush you back with a fast ball or throw one outside, and they're not going to miss by much either way. What makes them so good is that every time they throw a ball, they've got a purpose — not just to waste or throw over a hitter's head.

"A pitcher shouldn't throw a strike on an 0-2 count," says the man who has hit more than one such grooved toss out of the park. "But it should be close enough so that it gives a hitter something to think about."

Unlike other players, it's Hank's custom to carry his batting helmet with him up to the plate, rather than wear it before he gets there. It isn't that he dislikes it. "I like it all right; in fact, I love it," he said, recalling that if he hadn't been wearing a helmet, he might have been seriously injured on at least two occasions when hit by thrown balls. "The reason I don't put it on until the last minute is that it's heavy, and I want to make sure the pitcher's seeing me put it on," he added with a hearty chuckle.

He was hit in the head by two hard-throwing hurlers — Vernon Law of Pitts-

WIDE WORLD

Hank falls to ground after being hit by pitch thrown by Pirates' Vernon Law in 1959. His helmet has saved Hank from serious injury at least twice.

burgh, and, on a 3-0 count, Stan Williams of the Dodgers.

According to Hank, it's difficult to tell whether a pitcher ever hits a batter deliberately. There's such a small margin between a brushback pitch and a beanball. "A pitcher could be throwing up and in on a hitter, and the batter could be leaning over the plate guessing for something else, and be hit," Hank explained.

Henry's been thrown at over the years, especially in his first three or four seasons. "As a rookie, I guess, they sort of test you to see what kind of reaction you have." He remembers that after a couple of pitchers on one team — he thinks it was the Cardinals — had thrown at him a good deal, he made a statement that "the next time someone throws at me, I'm going to throw a bat or do something." He thinks now it was wrong to show the enemy that their tactics bothered him. "What I should have done," Hank says, "was not say anything, really. The best way to react is just to get up there and hit the daylights out of the next pitch. [Following his own advice, he's done exactly that.] That's the quickest way to eliminate the knockdown pitch, to show it doesn't bother you."

Good hitters, Henry included, aren't bothered that much by knockdown pitches, but there was a time in the 1969 season that he was really incensed. Dick Selma of the Cubs, supposedly "protecting" his hitters by retaliating against the Braves for knockdowns their hurler had thrown, pitched normally to two men up before Hank, but then "dusted" him off. Hank was angry: "It's not the idea of being thrown at. It's the idea of being singled out," he said.

What makes a good hitter? "Aggressiveness — knowing what you want to do when you get to the plate, what pitch you want to hit. Most good hitters — players like Stan Musial, Jackie Robinson, Frank Robinson, Ted Williams, Willie Mays — are aggressive at the plate," Hank said. "A player can help himself along as a hitter by not being lazy. The guy who stands there and waits for the pitch to be exactly down the middle, he's just not going to get those pitches in the big league."

Hank, who stands just a hair under six feet tall and weighs about 180 pounds of tightly coiled muscle, doesn't consider himself large, especially compared with some of the greats like Harmon Killebrew or Frank

Howard. "No matter how small you are, aggressiveness makes for good hitting."

In general, though, Hank said, "I respect" a pitcher for throwing a knockdown, providing the pitcher can control it. Don Drysdale used to throw inside on Hank a lot, enough to make him get away from the plate, but he never hit him (though Hank is sure Drysdale could have if he had wanted to).

"It's part of the game," Hank explained. "Some pitchers might want to waste an 0-2 pitch outside; some might on the inside. You've got to get out of the way." But: "If it hits you, it only hurts for a little while. Just shake it off and keep going."

There have been times when it seemed hitters would have a lot of shaking off to do — not from brushbacks, but from spitballs. "What's bad," said Hank, "is half the pitchers don't have control of it. They might throw one at your head, at your leg. That's the danger."

A spitball is difficult to hit, he added, because "you don't know which way it's going to break."

When Hank faces a pitcher for the first time, especially a young one, he might take as many as three pitches without swinging.

"I want to find out how his fast ball moves, how his slider breaks, how his curve ball breaks. He may strike me out the first time up, but I still want to know how his ball is moving, whether his fast ball is moving in on me or away from, if his curve ball is sharp enough, whether I've got to really concentrate on it. I don't want to look foolish on swinging at the first pitch." On the other hand, Hank said, there are times when he may swing at first pitches for a week. "It all works in cycles."

When Hank gets into a batting slump — and even the greatest hitters have them — he doesn't believe in taking extra hitting practice, especially if it's midseason. No matter how bad the slump, he said, he can hit one shot after another into the stands — in batting practice. "I don't think this is solving anything. The real concentration comes when you have to face that pitcher who's throwing live bullets. Showdown time is when that pitcher is throwing you good curves and good fast balls, and you don't know what's coming. *That's* the time you get yourself out of the slump."

A lot of good hitters preach that the way to overcome a slump is swing to hit through the middle, make sure your eye is on the ball.

Hank, whose batting average once dropped sixty-two points in two weeks, likes to go up there just with the idea of swinging.

One concession he may make is to use a heavier bat than usual. For at least fifteen years now, he's been using a thirty-four-ounce weapon, thirty-five inches long. (He started in the minors with a bigger-barreled one, then changed.) In a slump, he may pick up a thirty-five- or thirty-six-ounce bat, to slow his quick hands down and to keep his head from moving. "When I'm back in the groove, I pick up my regular bat again."

He's broken out of slumps spectacularly — once socking three homers, three doubles, and a single, in a twin bill. Supposedly that outburst followed printed reports that the enemy had found his weakness. Hank doubts it. "*I* don't even know my weakness," he said.

11

Records Are for Breaking

"A HOME RUN is the most exciting thing in baseball — I love to hit home runs."

That's what Hank Aaron says and that's what he has done, at the rate of better than thirty-five a year!

Of his many homers, his 1957 pennant-winning blast, described in Chapter Six, probably ranked highest in excitement. But there have been quite a few other memorable clouts along the way.

Proudest achievement was his 500th homer, a feat that up to that time only seven other players in the history of baseball had accomplished — Babe Ruth, Willie Mays, Mickey Mantle, Jimmy Foxx, Ted Williams,

Ed Mathews, and Mel Ott. (Ernie Banks joined the exclusive club later).

It happened in mid-July 1968. Hank had rapped numbers 498 and 499 in a single game, and his magic mark seemed just a few swings away. His father had come from Alabama to watch his son hit his 500th. Three days passed but Hank hadn't come close to hitting one into the seats, and Mr. Aaron went back to Mobile.

The next day, Sunday, July 14, was Peanut Day in Georgia, and there were enough baseball "nuts" on hand to make it the largest crowd of the season. The Braves were hosts to the San Francisco Giants. On the mound was Mike McCormick, the lefty who had won the Cy Young Award just the season before. In one game, Mike had made Bad Henry look *really* bad, striking him out three times on fast balls. On his first time up on Peanut Day, it looked as though McCormick was going to continue to overrun Hank. Then rain halted the game. Play was resumed, however, after nearly an hour, and in the second inning, with two on and two out, the count went to 3-1 on Aaron. McCormick delivered a belt-high fast ball — and Hank slammed it over the fence and off the Fan-O-Gram message board in left-center. (To-

Hank follows flight of his 500th home run with Giants' Jack
Hiatt and ump Bill Williams looking on. By the end of 1970,
Hank had hit 592 and was third in all-time homer derby.

day a white square marks the spot where Hank's historic homer struck.)

The game was halted for a home-plate ceremony, at which time Hank told his cheering fans, "I'm sorry I waited so long." Then the Braves crowned the day by winning the game 4-2.

Hammerin' Hank hit ten more homers before the 1968 season was over, added forty-four more in 1969, and then thirty-eight more the next year, bringing his total to 592 in 1970. Aaron was now moving into a really rare atmosphere, coming close to Willie Mays, who had 628 at the end of 1970, and Babe Ruth, whose lifetime total was 714.

Expected to slow down, Hank slammed forty-seven in 1971, the highest season's homer total he'd ever had. Then in 1972 he added thirty-four to bring his home run total to a super 673, surpassing Willie Mays' career output (654) to that point.

This gave him the second-best career home run total of anyone who ever played baseball, and put Hank in striking distance of the Babe Ruth record. Fans were soon talking not about *whether* Hank would break the seemingly unbreakable 714 record, but *when*. By June 12, 1973 Hank had added 16 more homers to his total; and every new home run he made during the 1973 season increased the excitement of sport fans. Hank felt the team and its location helped him.

"I'm playing in Atlanta, where the weather is ideal for me. It's not cold, even early in the season, and I'm cautious enough when we do run into some cool cities like San Francisco to take enough time to warm up. Atlanta Stadium is designed in such a way that if I hit a ball good — whether it's to right, center, or left — the ball will go out." (The stadium is 330 feet down each foul line and 400 feet through the center. The fence is six feet high.)

"More important, I've been fortunate to have great hitters around me in the lineup. With Orlando Cepeda and Rico Carty following me in the order, the pitchers were forced to pitch to me, instead of around me, as they would if I'd been the only long-ball hitter."

If Hank should fall short of the Babe's record by one homer, he could pin part of the blame on Bob Uecker, now a member of the Atlanta organization. Years ago, when Uecker was catching for the Cardinals, he continually needled the plate umpire about Hank. Uecker maintained that Aaron was stepping out of the front part of the batter's box when he swung. During one game,

Uecker complained a couple of times, and nothing was called. But, when Hank took a step toward the mound and hit a Curt Simmons change-up out of the park, the umpire called him out — for being out of the box.

The ump's decision made Hank angrier than he's ever been in baseball. "Still and all," Hank will admit now, "the umpire did what he thought was right. I'm sure if he had to make the same decision now, he'd probably call it the same way. I think the umpires have been very fair with me since I've been in the big leagues."

Not that Hank hasn't had his differences of opinion. Still, he seldom argues with the umpire even when he thinks an ump has called a strike on a pitch just like one he has just called a ball. Hank keeps his emotions under wraps, and he has never been thrown out of a game. "I believe I can't help my ball club, being thrown out. I feel I should stay in there and keep playing."

If Hank does break Ruth's record, some baseball fans may say, "You couldn't carry the Babe's boots." But if *he* doesn't break it, Hank says, someone else will.

"I hope so," he says, "just as I hope somebody will come along in the Braves' organization and break all *my* records. I wouldn't want my records to just stay in the books all the time. I'd like to see somebody break them. It means there's improvement."

It will be hard to improve upon Hank's records — or the thrills he's given the fans.

Many fans believe that Mister 44 wears a pair of lucky numbers, and certainly there have been a lot of events to bear this out. On June 8, 1961, four Braves, Ed Mathews, Hank Aaron, Joe Adcock, and Frank Thomas, set a major-league record, hitting four homers in a row against Cincinnati.

In four *games* in a row, Hank Aaron hit a four-bagger. From June 1 through June 4, 1967, he rammed his one-a-day medicine down the throats of St. Louis' Washburn, and Cincy's Ellis, McCool, and Maloney.

And if you want to carry the numbers game further, look at these facts: Hank has led his league in homers four times: In 1957 his forty-four four-baggers were tops in both leagues. In 1966 he led the National League with forty-four. In 1967, though, the numerology wasn't needed — Hank won with "only" thirty-nine. But in 1963 Hank tied for first place honors with Willie McCovey, who also wears number 44, and that is the exact number each of them hit that year. In 1969 Hank hit forty-four again, but Mc-

Covey didn't play the numbers game fair —
he hit one more, forty-five, to take the title.

During the years they were teammates,
Hank and Ed Mathews hit more home runs
combined (863) than any other duo in major-league history. This includes the Lou
Gehrig-Babe Ruth combo which accounted
for 793 circuit blows during the time they
played together.

In a game in June 1959, Hank came up
against San Francisco's Johnny Antonelli
with a man on, and homered. Five innings
later, he faced Stu Miller with a man on,
and homered; and the next inning, in the
same situation against Gordon Jones, Hank
homered!

That was the only time that he's hit *three*
homers in a single game. But by the start of
the 1971 season, he had hit *two* homers in a
game in forty-eight different games during
his baseball career.

One of Hank's greatest "home-run" hitting exhibitions came during batting practice before a game in Philadelphia. He
slammed a dozen in a row into the bleachers
or on the roof, as the fans gave him a stand-
ing ovation.

Hank has hit home runs in twenty different National League ballparks, including

the very first homer struck in Cincinnati's new Riverfront Stadium. He holds the National League record for most seasons (nine) for hitting at least one homer in every park.

New York's Polo Grounds has been torn down, but the memory of what Hank did there on June 18, 1962, still lingers on. From 1923 until that year, there had been only one verified instance (Joe Adcock in 1953) of anyone's hitting a ball in a major-league game into the distant center-field bleachers. Lou Brock, then a Cub rookie, somehow managed to do it on June 17, 1962. Then, the very next night, Hank faced Jay Hook *with the bases loaded* and exploded a drive to the left-center-field bleachers, more than 450 feet away.

His opening circuit blast of 1970 was a 503-foot clout that was the first upper-deck homer at Atlanta Stadium hit by a Brave or any right-handed batter. (Artist Wayland Moore marked the occasion by painting a hammer and the words "Aaron 557" on the seat where the homer landed.) The drive was Hank's first home at-bat of the year, his 557th career home run, and it moved him past Honus Wagner on the all-time RBI list.

"That's just about as hard as I can hit a ball," Hank remarked later, though he claimed he hadn't seen it land because he was concentrating on touching first base. "Touching first," Hank says, "is the first thing you worry about."

Hank has hit about an equal number of home runs on the road and at home. He's fair to all pitchers and more than 200 have been his victims.

Hank rates Don Drysdale among the toughest pitchers he's faced. Yet he's hit more homers off Drysdale (seventeen of them) than any other hurler. Hank's first homer off the Los Angeles ace was a grand-slam and on the same day, he drove in a fifth run with a single, went four-for-five, and stole a base, in a 10-5 Braves' victory.

If the great slugger loves to hit a home run, he's ecstatic about hitting a grand slam. "Anytime you're up with the bases loaded, you've got to dig in and give the best you have," says Henry, who thoroughly enjoys rising to a challenge.

Hank's first grand slam followed his pennant-winning blast in 1957. He hit two bases-loaded shots the next season, nine days apart. The first was off Muffett and the second off Drysdale. In 1961 he hit one slam, and the following year, struck three grand slams in the space of less than a month. Two of the three (including the mammoth Polo Grounds blast) were three days apart. After stroking two bases-full drives in 1963, he didn't hit another until 1966.

That was in New York on June 8, 1966, in a game against the Mets. Hank got the good wood on a Jack Fisher fast ball in the first inning and drove it over the fence. In the third, when Hank came up with a Brave at every sack, Fisher tried a slider. He shouldn't have because Hank hammered it out for a four-run blast. And in the sixth, Hammerin' Hank banged a double to right. He had defeated the Mets 7-6.

Grand slams in 1967, 1969, 1970, and 1972 brought Hank's total to fourteen, tying him at the time with Willie McCovey for the highest of any player still active. Number fourteen also took him past Ralph Kiner and Joe DiMaggio in this category. The late Gil Hodges also had fourteen grand slams. Still ahead were Babe Ruth (sixteen), Jimmy Foxx and Ted Williams (seventeen each), and all-time leader Lou Gehrig. Hank considers Gehrig's total of twenty-three out of his reach.

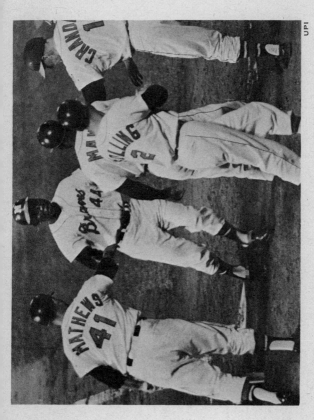

Ed Mathews and other teammates congratulate Hank on a 1963 grand-slam homer. Going into 1971, Hank's thirteen slams led active players.

12

Total Recall

AT THE END of a season, Hank can recall every one of his homers — and there's almost always more than thirty. He also remembers the pitcher he hit it off, and the kind of pitch it was, though he may not remember the game situation itself.

But there was one game in 1959 that he's probably never forgotten because he cost a teammate a home run. Harvey Haddix of the Pirates, in an incredible pitching performance, was hurling a perfect game against Milwaukee — and the game had gone into the thirteenth inning! In the bottom of the thirteenth, Felix Mantilla, safe on an error, was sacrificed to second, and Hank drew an intentional base on balls. Joe Adcock hit a towering drive over the right-field wall to rob Haddix of both the extra-inning no-hitter and the game. But Hank robbed Adcock of the homer, because in his joy, he cut across the field after touching second. He was ruled out, and Adcock was credited with a double.

Whether Hank goes up to the plate *trying* for a homer, depends on the situation. "When I go up in the ninth inning and we're behind by one run I know what my job is — to try to hit the ball out of the park. If we're two runs behind, I know my job is to try and get on base. Earlier in the game, if we're two or three runs behind, I'm going to try and get on base and get a rally started."

Many times, Hank has swung to get on base, just trying to meet the ball, and hit a four-bagger. "I think the time you hit a home run is when you're not expecting to."

Whether he'll swing for the seats on a 2-0 pitch, depends on the situation and who's pitching, Hank says. "If we're two runs behind, my object is to try to get on base. I won't try to swing on a 2-0 pitch because I can't hit a two-run home run with nobody on. It depends, too, on who's pitching. If the guy out there has control, like Marichal or

Gibson who don't walk too many, I might swing on 2-0, but not if it's a young kid out there. At least, I don't believe in it. What if you do hit a home run? You're still a run behind."

In a close game, when he *is* looking for a home run, Hank says he might take a pitch three times while he waits for the right one. In doing this, he runs the risk of being called out on strikes. But he estimates his number of strikeouts (1,214 in nineteen seasons) is about "par for the number of home runs I hit. I don't strike out as much as some of the real sluggers do. Mantle, for instance. He swung a lot harder than I do."

Through 1972, Aaron has had 1,190 career walks, among them 270 intentional ones. "You don't like to be walked, but there's nothing you can do about it."

It's been eight or nine years since he bunted. "It might be interesting to try," he has said. (Don't count on him to try, though.)

Three quarters of Hank's career home runs have been off right-handers. In the 1970 season, almost all of them were off righties. Part of his success is due to the fact that he faces a great many more right-handers than southpaws. Also, he thinks lefties get him out more because he's overconfident with them. "I think I bear down with right-handers a little bit more, wait a bit more."

Hank's record doesn't agree with the generally held belief that right-handed pitchers curb righty hitters. "I think a *good* hitter's going to hit regardless of whether a lefty or righty is pitching," Hank says. "Ted Williams hit both. So did Stan Musial, and look at Billy Williams."

Then what about those managers who platoon players, packing a line-up with left-handed hitters against right-handed pitchers? Hank feels that, "Some of the managers overdo it."

Early in his career, Hank could hit the ball as hard to right field as to left. In 1957, the year he was MVP, half of his home runs went to right field. One admiring pitcher commented that Hank could hit a pitch off his right ear into the right-field stands.

Nowadays Hank doesn't think it pays him to try to push to right. But he was still doing it when the team moved from Milwaukee to Atlanta in 1966. "I was so concerned about winning the fans, and the quickest way to do this is to hit the ball out of the park. So I went for the home run."

It didn't take him long to treat the Atlanta

fans to this Aaron specialty. Early in the season, April 20, 1966, he hit a pair of homers at Atlanta Stadium, the first of them off Ray Culp of the Phillies. Culp had also been the victim of the last home run Hank had hit at County Stadium, Milwaukee, the previous September.

Because Aaron has become so much of a pull hitter, several ball clubs go into a special shift against him.

It was either Gene Mauch or Harry Walker who started the anti-Hank maneuver, according to Aaron, and now Cincinnati, Pittsburgh, Chicago, Philadelphia, Montreal, and Houston use some special Aaron shift when the bases are empty.

"It doesn't bother me," Hank says. "In fact it makes me concentrate on hitting the ball a little harder. [Aaron, an opponent has said, "hits with fluid drive."] They want me to choke up and punch to right field to take away what I think is best, but I'm not that kind of a hitter. I've got to do the thing that I know I can do best. In the course of a season, it works to my advantage because if I hit a ball hard enough, it's going through, no matter what kind of shift is on."

Sometimes the shifts have taken hits or

extra bases away from Hank. At other times, they have worked to his advantage.

In Cincinnati he recalls, "They gave me the big gap in center. I hit a ball up the middle and Pete Rose was over to left-center. I took an extra base on him because I knew he didn't have a chance to throw me out." Hank slid in safely at second, and was singled home by Carty to tie the game. Aaron later hit a "soft" two-run homer to win the game 3-1.

In another game, after he homered against Montreal, the Expos' shift got him twice on ground balls behind second base. But then Hank singled through the spot the shortstop would normally have occupied, if the shift had not been on.

The most drastic shift used against Hank was fielded by Cincinnati in a game on June 30, 1969, when Manager Dave Bristol added a *fourth* outfielder against him. One inning, it was the second basemen who drew the spare outfield assignment; on another Aaron at-bat, the shortstop was sent out to pasture.

"I'll do anything to get Aaron out," Bristol explained, noting that a fourth outfielder enabled his left fielder to play closer to the line as a defense against balls heading for the corner. "It's not that you can always catch Hank's line drives, but maybe we can hold him to a single instead of a double."

In that game, the shift worked fine — up to a point. Three times Hank was retired easily. Then he hit the ball where even *five* outfielders couldn't have caught it. It was a three-run homer that sparked a 9-4 victory.

If Hank were setting up a defense against Henry Aaron, he'd play him as he would any other player — so he says. But he'd be wise to play him to pull — and deep.

13

Underrated Superstar

FROM the merciless way that Hank hammers pitchers, it is hard to think of him as being concerned about the welfare of an opposing hurler. But Hank always puts first things first, as he demonstrated in Chicago in 1970.

It happened when Hank was heading down the stretch toward his 3,000th hit. He had rapped a single (hit 2,992) to knock in the game's first run. Then he drilled a shot back at Cubs' pitcher, Joe Decker, that spun the hurler around.

Afraid that he had injured the young pitcher's throwing arm, Hank hurried over from first to say he was sorry. Although he was happy about adding to his hit totals, he was worried that his drive might have seriously hurt Decker, and possibly even put an end to his throwing career. "I want my hits," Hank says, "but the last thing I want is to hurt anyone." As it turned out, Decker was not seriously hurt, although he did not return to the game the next inning.

Later Hank added a third base knock against a relief pitcher. In the tenth, with Hank up and the score tied, reliever Archie Reynolds missed with a couple of curves, so Hank set himself for a fast ball. It came, and the Hammer nailed it to almost dead center for a homer to put the Braves ahead 7-6. It was the 2,995th hit and 568th four-bagger of Hank's career.

In that same series Ernie Banks hit *his* 500th career homer. When Hank congratulated him, Ernie said, "I'm just happy to be in the same category with you." Later Banks told a reporter. "I meant it. He's truly a great player."

One fan who listened avidly to broadcasts of Braves' games and cheered for Hank as he neared the 3,000-hit mark was Mrs. Paul Waner, widow of the great Pirate batsman.

Waner, who had been affectionately called "Big Poison" in his hitting heyday, served as the Braves' batting coach in Aaron's fourth year. Mrs. Waner was quoted as saying, "Paul once said that the one hitter who needed no help at all was a young man named Henry Aaron."

Ironically, it has taken years and years for the young man "who needed no help," to gain deserved recognition as a superstar. When fans wished Hank luck as he approached the 3,000-hit mark, he commented, "It's very nice to know that people know you're around."

"He was the most underrated ballplayer of my era," Mickey Mantle has said.

In Hank's early years, he played in the shadow of such greats as Spahn, Burdette, and Mathews. When they left, Hank was still "doing his thing," but the team wasn't winning pennants. Another factor may be that the team's franchise wasn't in a city like New York or Los Angeles, where the news and TV media are concentrated. And, as said before, Henry Aaron is a quiet professional. He doesn't kick over the traces, lose his temper in public, dress wildly, or affect a flamboyant style. But he is well liked and warmly admired. He's never let his fans down.

And Hank has had his days. His first "day" was actually a night, August 23, 1968, that featured the sale of Aaron Night souvenir buttons for the benefit of the Boys Club and the YMCA in the Atlanta area. Even the guest of honor paid for a button. Hank said about it: "I like kids, and as a ballplayer I think I can reach a lot of them where maybe other people couldn't."

Hank was also honored after his 3,000th base hit in May 1970.* At the ceremony in Atlanta Stadium, fans carried signs that read "We Love Henry" and "Hammerin' Hank Is Our Hero," and gave him a wild ovation. While Hank's proud family looked on, teammate Milt Pappas presented Hank with a silver hammer, and manager Luman Harris brought out a silver tray autographed by all his teammates. A parade of gifts followed — a fishing outfit, a year's supply of Coke, a personalized golf cart with "44" painted on the side, gas for 3,000 miles of driving, and a year's supply of dog food to go with a new French poodle. (The Aarons gave the dog away because of Princess, their Yorkshire terrier).

At the microphone, Paul Richards, VP of Baseball Operations, expressed what many people were thinking — that it was hard to

---

*Hoyt Wilhelm was also honored that day for his 1,000th game.

understand why Hank hadn't been named the athlete of the decade and number one on the all-time All-Star team.

Hank shyly and quietly expressed his thanks and said how wonderful it had been playing in Atlanta.

Bill Bartholomay, president of the Braves, replied, "Henry, thank *you* for the privilege of having been able to watch you."

There were other tributes to Hank. The State of Georgia honored him with a day in January 1970. And Morris Brown College has set up a Hank Aaron scholarship (four years of tuition and living expenses), and also a Hank Aaron Student Achievement Award, to which Henry has also contributed.

Hank says the award that is "the closest to my heart" is the one named for the late Ben Geraghty.

A special AP poll placed Hank fourth behind Koufax, Mantle, and Mays as the Athlete of the Decade.

Six times, Hank has been elected the most valuable Brave of the season and, in 1969, fans elected him the Greatest Brave of all time, an especially significant honor since he was chosen over such greats as Rabbit Maranville, Rogers Hornsby, Bob Elliott, Burdette, Spahn, and Mathews.

Hank appreciates his fans — especially

the young ones, for whom he feels a special affection. He says, "They're the people who come to see you."

Though Hank is applauded everywhere he goes, he is sometimes needled too. But usually it's good-humored kidding, like the banners that say, "Henry, you didn't have your Wheaties."

He doesn't mind that kind of needling. But once, in Chicago, at the height of the 1969 pennant race, a Cub fan threw beer at Hank, and Henry went after him.

When the Braves' franchise was moved from Milwaukee to Atlanta, Hank said he wouldn't take his children out of school and move them. He meant, not until the end of the school term. But some people misinterpreted this. They even said that Hank was threatening to quit baseball because of his concern about race prejudice in the South.

Hank knew what prejudice was like, from his own experience. He's been refused service in restaurants because of his color. He's had a policeman tail him through a Mississippi city because he was a black man driving a new car. He has endured taunts from fans in Florida.

However, as Hank says, "Atlanta's deep South, but playing here is like playing in

New York. It's a great place, a growing city. The people are nice, the fans are wonderful, and I've gotten along very well down here."

Although Hank doesn't think playing ball in Atlanta is any different than playing ball in Milwaukee, he does feel a special attachment to that Wisconsin city. "Fans in the early fifties in Milwaukee were the greatest fans in the world," he's said. "I kind of grew up with them. I came up in the big league as a kid, and I made mistakes in Milwaukee, and the people grew with me, and I grew with them."

As for Atlanta and the deep South, there are prejudiced people everywhere. Hank feels it's not worth wasting time or energy feeling anger toward them. "Anyway," he says, "the great majority of people who come to a ballpark come to see good, winning baseball. If you're good, they'll cheer you and like you whether you're black or white, and if you mess up they'll boo you and get on your back. That's the way it should be."

Hank is optimistic about the future of black-white relations, though he feels they will always be a problem "unless you spell it out to school kids." He believes schools and neighborhoods are the key. "If parents would leave their kids alone, they'd work out their problems," he says. "Get the kids playing together and eventually the grownups will mingle. Once you can get people mingling and talking and visiting each other, they'll be able to understand each other's problems and each other."

Early in Aaron's big-league career, when the Braves trained in Bradenton, Florida, the white ballplayers stayed downtown in a hotel, while the blacks had to settle for a rooming house about seven miles from the ballpark. Bill White, who was then playing with the Cardinals, came to Hank one year and said, "This is kind of silly for us to be staying in one place and the whites somewhere else." When Hank agreed, Bill said, "I'm going to my general manager and tell him," and Hank said, "I'll go and tell mine."

So Aaron told Birdie Tebbetts, who was the Braves' general manager at the time, that he was not satisfied with the way things were going.

"I think we should all be staying together," he said.

The next year, the training site was moved to West Palm Beach, Florida, where the owner of one hotel went against the usual discriminatory practice and let both black and white players stay in his hotel.

Hank feels baseball has been one of the great unifiers in American life, encouraging blacks and whites to play side by side in harmony. He believes that integration should be a goal of our society because, "It's good for the races to get together."

In all his baseball career, he's never been involved in a racial incident involving ballplayers. "All I want from a white ballplayer is respect," Hank says, "just as I respect him." But, "I'm not going to let anyone kick me without kicking back."

However, he is completely opposed to such forms of protest as looting and burning. He favors the nonviolent methods of the late Dr. Martin Luther King. Hank participated in a Dr. King memorial all-star baseball game for the benefit of the Southern Christian Leadership Conference, and wants to do more in the cause of civil rights.

He was shocked by a newspaper photo that appeared next to one of him being hoisted on his teammates' shoulders after his 1957 pennant-winning homer. The second picture showed police dogs snapping at Negro children in a Southern town. "I never got that contrast out of my mind," Hank said. "With different breaks I could have been one of the kids facing the dogs."

Someone has suggested to him that just being Hank Aaron, performing with excellence and being a credit to the game both on and off the field, was in itself an important contribution to racial unity. "My theory about that, though," he replied, "is that as long as you don't ask for anything, it seems as if you're satisfied, and you're not going to get anything."

14

Captain Henry and
the 1969 Season

BEFORE the 1969 season began, Hank was named team captain. The appointment was a tribute to his leadership qualities, especially with younger players. According to Don Davidson, the traveling secretary of the Braves, the young ballplayers gather around Hank the way "chicks do around a mother hen." "But what is remarkable," says Mark Gladulich, the equipment manager of the Atlanta club, "is the way the Hammer seeks out the newcomers."

"I try to stay as close to them as I can," says Hank, remembering his own lonely, frightened days as a baseball rookie. "I feel I can work with them, help them out. I like

"Captain Henry" Aaron playfully inspects the "weapons" of teammates (left to right) Ken Johnson, Tito Francona, and Bob Tillman in Braves' clubhouse.

to see a young kid come along and make progress."

Take Hal King's experience, for example. The Braves' young catcher told a sportswriter in May 1970 that, though he was seeing the ball all the way, he was having trouble making contact with it and he had no idea why.

Then "The Hammer came over to me one day and asked if he could make a suggestion," King relates. "Asked! Can you imagine Henry Aaron *asking* if he could make a suggestion to me? He's some kind of all-right guy, on and off the field. He always has time to help you, if he can.

"Well, anyway, he said he'd been observing me at the plate and thought he'd caught something that might help. Said I might try it, just to see what I thought."

Hank suggested that King use a heavier bat than the thirty-three-ounce toothpick he'd been using. And he also suggested that the catcher try to be more patient at the plate.

"So if I ever do much of anything good as a hitter, you ought to give Hammer more of the credit. He's some kind of guy."

Some kind of guy is right. Mark Gladulich told a reporter: "Henry is the one the whole team has the real great respect for. It's just that he's so quiet and so modest that unless you watch him over a long period of time, you don't realize what a strong, deep influence he has."

The young players watch Hank's swing, his reaction to different pitchers, his moves. They know, said the equipment manager, that "he's always there when you need him to answer questions about hitting, fielding, base-running, or personal problems. Hank is a good listener. He will laugh at the younger players' jokes, and make them feel wanted. He creates a whole kind of family mood that's especially valuable when things aren't going so well."

Gladulich, who has been close to many players over a long period of time, went on to say, "Nobody has set such a consistently high standard of conduct on and off the field."

Gladulich expresses an opinion that most baseball people share about Hank: "A kind of credit to baseball and to manhood, the sort of fellow everyone can look up to, and feel proud of."

Hank felt honored to be named captain, a title no one on the Braves had held for several seasons. When Hank was appointed, he told his teammates that they all had a share in the honor accorded him.

Aaron's opponents, too, respect his knowledge and abilities. Johnny Bench, sensational catcher for the Cincinnati Reds, says that opposing players gather to watch Hank in batting practice. "He doesn't even swing, it seems, and he just sends it out with a flick of the wrist."

Yet Hank Aaron himself says he's never been satisfied with a season since he began playing the game.

This is from a man who has hit as high as .355, had 223 hits, knocked in 132 runs, and rapped as many as 400 total bases. But Hank says, "When you get satisfied, you get complacent." And complacent is one thing Henry never wants to be.

The seasons that have caused him the most dissatisfaction are those in which he scored less than one hundred runs and drove in fewer than one hundred. "Those are the two departments, I think, where you help the club most. Every year when I go to spring training, those are the two things I want to accomplish." Aside from his freshman year, the only seasons Hank dropped below a hundred in runs scored were 1968, 1971, and 1972. They were otherwise generally good years, though. In 1971 he walloped 47 four-baggers, hit .327, and knocked in 118 runs with 162 hits.

ATLANTA BRAVES

Hank bowls over Cards' catcher, Tim McCarver, to score on a
sacrifice fly in 5-3 Braves' victory during the 1969 race.

At the opening of the 1969 season — a season that will be long remembered as the Year of the Mets — Hank was eager to prove that he could come back and have a good year.

He started out like a house on fire.

In May he was hitting a sizzling .389, just a point behind the Mets' Cleon Jones. On May 15, Hank clouted two homers and got a third hit as the Braves edged the Mets 6-5. A week later, when fortunes were reversed and the Mets slaughtered Atlanta 15-3, Hank was removed for a pinch-hitter for the second time in his career. He had already whacked a single and four-bagger. Mike Lum, who hit for him, doubled.

Late in May, the Braves opened a four-game lead in the Western Division. It was the biggest lead they'd hold all season, but at the time it looked as though they had their best chance for a championship since losing in a play-off ten years earlier.

Against the Pirates in early June, Hank's 525th career homer — the fourth in a week — broke a 10-10 tie, and pushed him past Ted Williams by four. The Braves' sweep of the double-header put them ahead by two games.

When Hank's eighteenth homer of the

season beat the Astros in the final inning, he cracked: "I had to hit it in the ninth to keep the game from going into extra innings. I don't get paid for overtime."

Again and again, Hank showed his wonderful instinct for predicting pitches. Late in June, the Braves were locked in a 3-3 tie with the Dodgers. In two at-bats, Hank had been thrown fast balls by Claude Osteen. This time, Osteen thought Hank might be guessing fast ball again, so he threw him a curve and Hank homered to break the tie.

The Braves won 5-3, and for a day, they took a half-game lead in the Western Division. After the game, Osteen was quoted as saying about Hank, "I can think of many things more enjoyable than getting careless with him — including slapping rattlesnakes."

At the time of the All-Star Game, the Braves were leading the division by a game. In the first game after the All-Star Game, Hank homered for the first time on a pitch he couldn't figure out. It was his 535th and it put him in fourth place behind Mantle in the all-time home-run derby. The next day, Hank walloped his twenty-sixth of the season to tie Mickey.

He passed Mantle with 537 the same

week he got his 2,900th base hit and moved into sixth place in total bases. The homer came in a Brave victory in which catcher Bob Tillman had three home runs. At last people began talking about Hank as a record-breaking hitter.

The next day the Braves started on a five-game losing streak that dropped them to third, but they bounced back. Against the Phils, Hank rapped two homers and a single to bring his team within five percentage points of the Reds, and to enable him to pass the legendary Ty Cobb for all-time extra-base hits.

The Braves lost five of their next six and were now in fifth place. Five clubs were bunched within two games of first place.

On August 19, Ken Holtzman of the Cubs was holding the Braves hitless when Hank came up in the seventh and hit a towering drive to left. He was sure the ball was going in. The trouble was the wind held it back just long enough for Billy Williams to make a great catch against the ivy. Holtzman finished with a no-hitter. The Cubs won 3-0, and the Braves, still in fifth place, were now 3½ games behind. It was their twenty-eighth loss in forty-seven games.

The Braves were worried. Orlando Cepeda suggested having a meeting. Hank agreed and called the players together for a secret session. It was short and sweet, a quiet rally at which "we decided we were good enough to win."

The "rally" worked like a tonic as the Braves took the next two games from the Cubs, dropped a close one to Gibson in St. Louis, and then won five in a row. They were now just a half game away from the top.

In that fifth victory, Hank banged in six of his club's eight runs with a grand slam and a two-run homer against the Pirates. The slam was his twelfth, tying him with Banks.

All this time, a floating bone chip and calcium deposits in Hank's back were causing him so much pain he sometimes had to take pills to sleep. But he didn't talk about it, unless someone asked. Pain and all, he was staying in the line-up.

His home-run rampage continued. On September 10, when the Braves played host to the Giants, Hank hit his fortieth of the season, and Atlanta beat San Francisco 8-4. The following day, Hank swatted his forty-first, while the Giants' Willie McCovey, the league leader, hit two (his forty-third and forty-fourth). With the score tied at three all, Mike Lum hit a bases-loaded single to give the Braves a 5-3 victory. Now Atlanta was one percentage point out of first; the Giants had dropped to third. When the Braves extended their win streak with three in a row over the Astros, they got the go-ahead signal to print tickets for the pennant play-offs.

Everybody chipped in with his best performance. It might be Rico Carty or Tony Gonzalez or Orlando Cepeda hitting a game-winning homer. Or Felix Millan (now with the New York Mets) having a four-hit night. Hank consistently played a key role in the division championship drive — with the big clutch hit, or great catch and throw, or heads-up hustle (for example, when he was given a base on balls and made it to second on the ball-four pitch that got away).

In one game, Hank broke for second, but his possible steal was wiped out when Carty homered. "He wasn't supposed to hit it," a reporter suggested. Hank, grinning, corrected him: "He wasn't supposed to hit it *that hard.*"

Later in the game, Henry clouted one of his own.

15

The Best in the West
Meets the Best in the East

IT WAS a very hot race!

On September 10, 1969, the Braves, Giants, Reds, Dodgers, and Astros had been bunched within two games of one another in the Western Division. A week later, the Braves, Giants, and Dodgers were in first place at *different times of the same day!*

On the morning of September 17, the Giants were in first place. That afternoon, though, they lost to Houston, and the Dodgers took over top spot — by one/one-hundredth of a percentage point. And they could hold on to their precarious lead only if they beat the Braves that night.

In that contest, a sloppy affair, Hank

broke an oh-for-sixteen hit famine with a harmless single and added another safety during a rally that tied the game at three all. It was five all when Hank came to the plate in the twelfth. Dodger rookie Ray Lamb got away with two fast balls. He came in with a third. With the snap and crackle of a buggywhip, Hank's wrists plunged the bat into the ball and popped it 425 feet into the Dodger bullpen. The Braves, with the 6-5 win, moved into first place, the third team to hold that spot that day.

Possession lasted just one day, as the Dodgers turned the tables. The Braves moved next into San Diego, whose Padres had taken three of four games with the Dodgers and Giants. Atlanta swept the Padres and stayed within half a game of the division leaders. Hank's forty-third circuit clout, on a relief pitcher's first throw, helped in one of the victories.

Following their three in a row over San Diego, the Braves repeated their act in Houston. The first victory over the Astros was highlighted by a case of mistaken identity. A Houston runner on third (and just about everyone else in the park) mistook Braves' catcher Bob Didier's plastic finger guard for the ball, as the guard flew back to the barrier. Norm Miller, the baserunner who had reached third on a Cecil Upshaw wild pitch, thought it was another wild pitch, and scooted homeward. But Didier had the ball all the time, and Miller was an easy out in a rundown to retire the side.

The second win over Houston — in which Hank had a double and a single and knocked in a pair of runs — eliminated the Astros from contention and moved the Braves back to first by half a game.

The third victory — in which Hank rapped three hits — coupled with a Giant loss expanded the Braves' lead to 1½ games, with just five games left to play.

Back home, the Braves were hosts to the Padres, winning another trio — a total of nine victories in a row. Hank hit number forty-four in a game in which Braves' hurler Phil Niekro was pitted against his brother Joe, who was on the mound for the Padres. In that game, Cepeda hit a grand slam, Boyer socked on a solo shot, and Millan had four hits.

With just two games left on their schedule, the Braves were a virtual shoo-in for the division title. Only if they were to lose both their remaining games and the Giants were to win all three of theirs, could Atlanta possibly be done out of the National League Western Division championship.

More than 46,000 fans were there to watch the Braves try for the clincher against the Reds, who had been eliminated three days earlier. Hank, trailing McCovey (his choice for MVP that season) by a single homer for the league leadership, declared: "I've got more exciting things to worry about, like winning a championship. I'd like to win the homer crown, but I'd gladly trade it for the division title."

He got his wish.

Against Cincinnati, the Braves pulled out in front in the third on a single by Niekro, Millan's sacrifice, a dribbler by Gonzalez, and Hank's single. The Reds came back with two runs; but the Braves rallied, and Carty's bases-loaded line drive, on which Pete Rose made a sensational catch, was enough to drive across the run that put the Braves ahead 3-2.

In the ninth, Lee May struck out, but Atlanta hearts skipped a beat when Jimmy Stewart, the Reds' left fielder, drove one deep to right field. Aaron went back and back and hauled the ball in at the fence, only a few feet short of Homerville.

That left just one out to go. Hoyt Wilhelm, who had come in to pitch after Niekro was lifted for a hitter, threw. Alex Johnson hit a grounder to Bob Aspromonte, who tossed to Cepeda for the final out. It was Wilhelm's fourth save in six games — and the Braves had made it. They were "the best in the West."

Fans rushed on the field to mob their heroes, who were jumping about in delight. Chief Noc-A-Homa,* the Braves' Indian "mascot," hurried to take down his left-field teepee, which was under police protection from souvenir-hunters. In the clubhouse, Carty, who had made a game-saving shoe-string catch, danced to the tune of "Oh Happy Day."

Carty had had a great stretch performance; so had Cepeda, Gonzalez, and others. And what about Aaron? Dave Bristol, the Reds' manager that year, put it in a few choice words: "I've never seen one like him. He rises to the occasion."

The next occasion to which Hank and his

---

*Chief Noc-A-Homa, whose real name is Levi Walker, Jr., is a full-blooded Indian of the Algonquin nation. Before his job with the Braves, he was an insurance agent. In celebration of a home run, he will sometimes create smoke signals above his teepee with a smoke bomb.

teammates would try to rise would be the National League pennant play-offs. They were going against the so-called "Team of Destiny," the New York Mets. Whichever team won three games first would make it to the World Series.

"We all went in expecting to win," Hank recalls, "but I never underestimated the Mets, who had as good a team as anybody in the league."

Hank felt Gil Hodges, late manager of the 1969 "Impossible Dream," had done a "tremendous job" with some of the younger players. In addition, Hank said, the Mets had a great pitching staff, capable of throwing shutouts, and were otherwise strong down the middle with Jerry Grote behind the plate, Ken Boswell at second, Bud Harrelson, "one of the best," at shortstop, and Tommie Agee in center field. In Hank's judgment, Agee (now with Houston) had developed into a truly fine center fielder.

The Mets were "strong where they had to be strong" and Hank, for one, was not taking them for granted.

But the Hammer, who had nailed down a division championship, went into the best-of-five play-offs with a handicap: a painful injury he got while trying to free the family's German shepherd from a fence. The dog's claws raked the back of his right hand and little finger, and he needed a dozen stitches plus pregame shots.

The Mets' Tom Seaver faced Phil Niekro in the opener at Atlanta Stadium before a crowd of 50,122. The Mets were leading 2-1 when in the third, Millan and Gonzalez doubled to get one run back. Hank followed by knocking in the go-ahead tally with a hit he turned into a double by side-stepping the Mets' astonished second baseman. After the Mets got back the lead in the fourth, Gonzalez tied it with a homer in the fifth. It was four-apiece in the seventh when Hank hammered a fierce homer to left. But then the Mets charged back with five runs in the eighth inning to wrap up the ballgame.

More than 50,000 fans showed up for the second play-off game, a Sunday afternoon in Atlanta, with Mrs. Martin Luther King throwing out the first ball. On the mound, the Braves used six different hurlers. In $4\frac{1}{2}$ innings, New York jumped off to a 8-0 lead with homers by Agee and Boswell and led 9-1 going into the bottom of the fifth. With two men on, Hank walloped a homer past the 400 mark in deep center, and the Braves tallied five that inning to get back in the game.

But Atlanta hopes died quickly. Tommie Agee, who had just missed having his head taken off by a Cleon Jones foul liner when he tried to steal home on his own, rode in on Jones' homer. The 11-6 score held up, and the Braves were within a single game of being eliminated.

The do-or-die third play-off game was played in New York's Shea Stadium before a crowd of 53,195. Pat Jarvis was on the mound for the Braves, against the Mets' Gary Gentry. In the Braves' first, after Gonzalez singled, Hank smacked a four-bagger — the third game in a row in which he'd hit one. Agee's second homer of the series got one back for the Mets in the third.

The next inning, New York went ahead when Art Shamsky singled and Boswell homered. It looked like more trouble when Ed Kranepool doubled, but an Aaron-to-Millan-to-Boyer relay cut him down trying to stretch it to a three-bagger. In the fifth, Atlanta picked up a pair of runs when Cepeda homered after Carty walked. Atlanta's 4-3 lead was short-lived, though. In the Mets' half of the inning, Garrett (who had been drafted from a Braves' farm team) homered with Ryan on; Jones doubled and was singled home by Boswell to make it 6-4 Mets. New York added an insurance run in the sixth on a Grote double, a sacrifice, and an Agee single.

Ironically, a double by Hank in the third inning may have proved fatal to the Braves. For Hank's base knock, sending Gonzalez to third, helped send starter Gary Gentry to the showers. The count went to 1-2 on Rico Carty, the next batter, and Nolan Ryan was summoned from the bullpen. Ryan struck Rico out, walked Cepeda intentionally, fanned Boyer, and got Bob Didier on a fly to left. Ryan went on to get two hits, score a run, keep the Braves in check, and set them down in order in the ninth. The "best in the East" had defeated the "best in the West." The incredible Mets were National League champions.

After the game, Atlanta skipper Luman Harris told the Braves they had nothing to be ashamed of. Hank, especially, had distinguished himself (except for one harmless fielding lapse when he threw a ball to the infield where no one was waiting to catch it, and the runner who had singled was able to advance to second.)

Hank, with five hits (three homers and

Hank pounded out a homer in each of the three National League pennant play-off games that the Braves lost to the New York Mets in 1969. He batted a sizzling .357.

two doubles) in fourteen at-bats, hit .357, tying him with Agee, but not series high. Aaron's three homers, one in each game, were the most anyone had, and he led in RBI's by batting in seven of the Braves' fifteen play-off tallies.

His season's totals included a .300 batting average, 100 runs scored, 97 RBI's, and 44 homers. Hank's 332 total bases were tops in the league. He had 30 doubles and three triples among his 164 hits.

In the balloting for Most Valuable Player, Hank finished third behind Tom Seaver and Willie McCovey, the winner.

After their victory, Mets' manager Gil Hodges commented: "I don't believe enough can be said about Henry Aaron. You don't see a thirty-five-year-old man with such quick wrists, who can still run and throw, and do everything so well. When you speak of real outstanding players, his name doesn't come up as quickly as it should, but it does when pitchers talk about great hitters."

It was interesting that Hank, with his forty-four regular-season home runs plus his three in the play-offs in 1969 equaled the number he had hit (forty-four during the regular season, plus three in the World Series) as a twenty-three-year-old back in 1957.

As Hank was getting ready to catch a plane after the Braves' loss to New York, one of the Baltimore Orioles' scouts tried to get some inside information on some of the Met players, but Hank — out of loyalty to his league — wouldn't give any.

The scout said, "I don't think they're going to handle us as well as they handled you."

Hank replied, "Well, that's your problem. It's not mine anymore."

As everyone knows, the Mets beat the Orioles in the World Series, four games to one. Baltimore scored fewer runs against the Mets in five games than the Braves had in three games. One reason the Orioles lost the 1969 World Series, in Hank's opinion, is that they underestimated the New York Mets.

16

Talent Isn't Enough

JOHNNY BENCH says Hank Aaron's statistics are "unbelievable," and indeed they are. (See the Appendix for his lifetime records.) Those records are built on a number of factors: Hank's quiet competitive fire, his jet-quick hands, the effortless, ferocious flick of his murderous wrists.

Paul Richards says that Hank wins games not only with his bat, legs, and arm — but with his head. Intelligence is "very important," according to Hank, who still studies the game and concentrates all the time. "I think if you've got a ballplayer who's kind of hard-headed, who doesn't learn, doesn't pick up things quickly, he isn't going to make it in the majors, even if he has a world of talent."

In Hank's opinion, the less talented player who learns quickly will get to the big leagues sooner than the more talented one who refuses to learn and acts as if he knows everything.

Aaron has seen young pitchers make the same mistakes until it's embarrassing. On the other hand, he admires those young ballplayers who use their heads. He mentioned teammate Oscar Brown as an example. In 1970 Brown's ninth-inning bunt with two strikes moved a runner along, and set the stage for a game-winning homer by Hammerin' Hank against the Mets. Oscar bunted because he wanted to avoid an inning-ending double-play. The Braves were a run behind at the time.

"I like to see plays like that," Hank says. "I like to see a ballplayer thinking. Felix Millan thinks all the time at the plate. He knows what he's got to do."

What a ballplayer has to do specifically depends to an extent on his place in the batting order.

"You've got to have a pretty good lead-off man, but from second to fifth in the order is where you're going to win ballgames," says Hank. He's hit clean-up, fifth, and second at different times, but for most of his years in the big leagues, he's been third in the order. "I'm very proud to be hitting where I am. I feel like the managers have given me a responsibility," he said.

What should a number three hitter be able to do for his club?

"If he has anybody hitting behind him at all, he's got to score one hundred runs. He's also got to bat in one hundred runs. And he's got to get on base. He's got to hit .300 or close to it. He's got to be a fearsome object at the plate," says the Hammer, whose hitting talents have overshadowed his other skills.

Hank admits that he's stolen his share of enemy signs and flashed them to batters on his club, but when he's up at bat he relies on his own judgment. He's never taken a sign from an opposing player, for a very practical reason: "You don't have to miss but one time, and you're ducking your head into a fast ball. And it's all over."

There are coaches who have just about made a "career" of sign-stealing, but Hank's still not having any.

Coaches, incidentally, were once the target of Hank's ire. A runner from second was held up at third after a hit in an early inning. Hank thought the coach was overly cautious and should have sent the runner home. Hank told reporters the coaches were spending too much time on foolish things like bedchecks and not paying enough attention to their on-field duties. "I'm the kind of a guy who says what's on his mind," Hank said at the time.

Whenever Hank talks about new players of the future, he can't help thinking of the great ones of the past. Asked to name the best players he's played with or against, Hank offers this all-National League squad:

CATCHER	Del Crandall
FIRST BASE	Willie McCovey
SECOND BASE	Jackie Robinson
SHORTSTOP	Bobby Wine
THIRD BASE	Ed Mathews or Clete Boyer
LEFT FIELD	Stan Musial
CENTER FIELD	Willie Mays
RIGHT FIELD	Roberto Clemente

PITCHERS	Warren Spahn
	Sandy Koufax
	Juan Marichal
	Don Drysdale
	Bob Gibson
	Tom Seaver
MANAGER	Walter Alston

"I think I could win a pennant with that ball club," Hanks says laughing at his own understatement.

Then he goes on to explain his selections: He picked Del Crandall, his old teammate, "more as a smart catcher than as a hitter. Many backstops are better hitters — Johnny Bench, for instance — but Crandall had all the tools. He didn't have a great arm, but he had an accurate arm. Nobody stole on him that much; he could throw anybody out."

Dick Allen is Hank's second choice for first sacker, but he gave the nod to Willie McCovey because of his experience.

He had no hesitation making his choice of Jackie Robinson. He picked Bobby Wine at short because "though he doesn't hit much, I like his glove. He can be a great asset to a ball club. If he played on a pennant winner, he'd be a much better hitter."

For third base, Hank said he was torn between Ed Mathews, unquestionably the better hitter, and Clete Boyer, "probably the greatest fielding third baseman in either league." Hank thought awhile and then added, "I know they talk a lot about Brooks Robinson, but I don't think *anybody* can play third like Clete could. Everytime I'd see Clete, he'd be making a fantastic play."

The choice Hank would make between Eddie and Clete would largely depend on the make-up of the rest of the team. If it was a strong hitting club, Hank would go with Boyer. If it needed a good man with the wood, he'd go with Mathews.

The men he picked for the outfield "wouldn't embarrass anybody," Hank said. "I still have a lot of respect for DiMaggio, but Mays in his prime was the greatest center fielder *I* ever played against."

Walter Alston was Hank's choice for manager because Walter has done well with all types of teams, the pitching types, slugging types, running types. "I think he can cope with just about anything."

When it comes to the rising stars of the

National League, Hank sees a number of them: Johnny Bench, Most Valuable Player twice; Bobby Bonds of San Francisco; and Oscar Brown, Dusty Baker, and Ralph Garr on the Braves, are among those likely to develop into great players. Some other up-and-coming youngsters that Hank likes are the Pirates' second baseman, Dave Cash; Houston's center fielder, César Cedeno; and the Cards' Bernie Carbo. Among pitchers, he predicts stardom for Wayne Simpson and Jim McAndrew.

"I've seen more good-lookin' kids come up to the league in the past several years than I've seen in a long time."

These stars eventually may join Dick Allen (and Hank himself?) on the list of players earning $200,000 a year. Hank agrees that Johnny Bench, the young Reds' star, is a likely candidate. But he feels several others could also qualify — the National League's Billy Williams, Tom Seaver, and Bobby Bonds are possibilities. In Hank's opinion, "to qualify for that kind of money, a ballplayer's got to do so many things. Billy Williams, I'd nominate right now. He only plays one position but he plays it so well. He plays every day. Every year he hits .300, bats in one hundred runs, scores one hundred runs and he's out there every day. An iron man."

At the $200,000 level or below, today's money situation for ballplayers is very different than it was when Hank started out. He remembers the end of that season in the minors when Jacksonville fans passed around a hat to collect extra money for their low-paid players. In the sixties, Hank was particularly gratified to become a member of the $100,000-a-year club, not only for the money, but because it put him in the category of such great stars as Williams, Mantle, DiMaggio, Mays, Musial, and Clemmente. He feels that ballplayers aren't paid that much money unless owners think they're worth it, and that black players, especially, have to wait long to be recognized — fifteen years in his own case. He adds, "Players like Pete Rose, who hit two hundred singles, get that much; my two hundred hits have to include forty home runs to get that much."

Some people charge that the quality of baseball has been lowered because players "aren't hungry enough" anymore. Hank doesn't think this is true. He feels players are underpaid, considering their road expenses, and he's glad to see athletes investing in enterprises to take care of themselves after they leave the sport.

Hank, himself, has various investments, including a share in the Braves' all-sports camp near Clayton, and he was briefly owner of a barbecue restaurant in Atlanta.

For a year-and-a-half, Hank was a sportscaster on WQXI-TV in Atlanta. In addition to giving the scores of football and basketball games, he'd comment on baseball and other sports (usually ad lib) and interview prominent athletes. "It's not as easy as it looks," Hank says about having to stand up and talk into a TV camera. Just the same, he enjoyed his broadcasting experiences.

17

Changing Times

"WHEN I first came into baseball I had a taste for it that has never changed. I still love to play though it gets harder with the length of the schedule, the traveling, and the night games."

Hank would like to see the season shortened to about 150 games. He's confident the result would be better baseball.

"People go out to the ballpark to see you play your best. They're paying top dollars to see top ballplayers, but when you're traveling the way we did [from Los Angeles to San Diego to Houston for two days each and then back to the West Coast for two days], it's impossible to perform your best."

Though he thinks the regular season should be shortened, Hank is in favor of keeping pennant play-offs, so that fans can see more excitement-packed games with a championship at stake.

He also considers expansion of the major leagues a good thing: "Some people are complaining that there are too many teams in the majors, but expansion has given some good players an opportunity to play more. Look at a ball club like San Diego. The Padres have Clarence Gaston, who used to be on the Braves. He hit about .318 in 1970. He was with our organization for several years before that, but he never got a chance to play. If expansion hadn't come along, he'd still be buried in the minors."

Hank is interested in several rule changes that have been suggested. One change, already adopted by the American League, allows a pitcher a man to pinch hit through the game without taking the field. The man he pinch hits for doesn't have to leave the game. The idea was tried out in spring training, and Hank, as a designated pinch-hitter, got several hits, including a homer. "It would be great if they'd let me hit and let somebody else do the chasing," he laughs.

Hank would also like to see the distances

to the fences made uniform in all parks. This would do away with teams adjusting distances to suit the sluggers on their club.

When pitching mounds were ordered lowered, Hank was all for the change for several reasons. For one thing, he said "Pitchers can't fall off the mound [for extra momentum behind their pitches] the way they used to. . . . Also it's changed the pattern of the strike zone a little. And, sliders used to break a lot more sharply than they do now — it's made them flatter." Hank sums it up: "Whatever hurts the pitcher helps the hitter, so the lowered mound has to help me."

What may hurt *all* players, in Hank's opinion, is the artificial turf that the Astrodome and other parks are using. He predicts that all parks will have it sooner or later because of the easy maintenance. But he says if he plays four games in the Astrodome, his whole leg aches. According to Hank, the use of artificial turf "is going to shorten a lot of ballplayers' careers because it's so tough on the legs."

More than one slugging outfielder has been moved to first base in his later years as a way of extending his career; for example, Stan Musial and Mickey Mantle.

Hank Aaron has played first base at different times over the past few seasons. In fact, he played there in 109 games in 1972. But he feels most comfortable in the outfield, where he played more than 2,500 major league games through the 1972 season. Before that, there had been considerable speculation that he would wind up his career as his team's first sacker. But in 1973 he was back in the outfield, apparently to stay. One concession to his years was that he moved to left field. Because he is closer to third base in left field, there isn't as much throwing pressure.

For the Braves, 1970 was a very disappointing season. With pitchers Cecil Upshaw and Ron Reed sidelined by injuries, they ended in fifth place in the West, winning seventy-six games and losing eighty-six, for a .469 average.

As always Hank was more interested in the Braves' winning than in his own statistics. But as disappointed as he was with the team's showing, 1970 held some satisfactions for Hank — his 3,000th hit, his thirteenth grand slam, his tape-measure drive at Atlanta Stadium. In 1970, too,

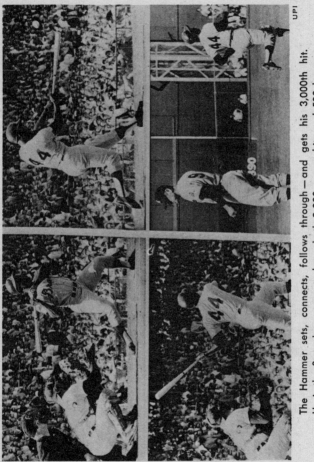

The Hammer sets, connects, follows through—and gets his 3,000th hit.
He is the first player ever to have both 3,000 career hits and 500 homers.

Hank moved into fourth place on the list of the all-time extra base hitters and seventh place on the all-time RBI roster. His 118 runs-batted-in marked the tenth year he'd passed one hundred, tying him with Mays and Musial for a National League record, which he broke the next season.

Hank led in the All-Star Game balloting among fans throughout the United States and Canada. "I'm grateful," he said. "I feel honored that people all over voted for me."

Hank was his club's leading clutch hitter, based on how often he batted in the game-winning or game-leading run and hit with men in scoring positions. He ended the season with a .298 average, 103 runs scored, and 118 runs-batted-in to go with his 38 home runs.

A highlight of the 1970 season was an eleven-game Braves' winning streak, in which Hank walloped six homers, the last three of them hit to right, right-center, and dead center.

In a victory against the Cardinals, Aaron smacked a pair of homers, hitting his first on a 1-2 count. The 0-2 pitch he had let go for a ball was so close that the outraged catcher forgot to throw to second to prevent a steal. Hank's second homer broke a 6-6 deadlock.

The score of one game made it seem more like a football contest than baseball. The Pirates beat the Braves 20-10, and the combined run total and the number tallied by the Pirates were each records.

In the course of the game, Hank struck his twenty-ninth and thirtieth home runs, making it twelve seasons in which he walloped thirty or more — a National League record. His second circuit clout of the game was followed by a Rico Carty homer. In the top of that same inning, Bob Robertson, Willie Stargell, and José Pagan had hit consecutive homers for the Pirates. The five four-baggers tied a record for homers hit by two clubs in a single inning.

Hank also had a third hit and five RBI's, and cut off a ball in the alley that might have been an inside-the-park homer.

The season was also marked by a home-plate collision between Hank and Dick Dietz, the Giants' catcher, when Hank tried to score from second without sliding. "I wasn't trying to kick the ball out of his hand," Hank said afterward. "He had the plate pretty well blocked, and the only way I could get to the plate was to try and run

over him. So he gave me a little of his hip
and I caught my right leg behind his knee
somehow and I was flipped through the air.
I was really dizzy."

The resulting knee injury kept Hank out
of action two or three days. He is still bothered by it and the development of a baker's
cyst, which has to be drained.

In 1971, the Braves finished in third place
with an 82-80 record. Hank had a superb
year, passing the 600 career home-run mark
in April against Gaylord Perry of the Giants
in Atlanta Stadium. "It would have been
sweeter if we'd won," he commented, then
added, "I'd like to be remembered as a good
all-round hitter, not just a fellow who hit
home runs. . . . I like to look at myself as a
complete ballplayer." Hank's 47 homers that
year was his highest season's total.

In 1972, the Braves wound up fourth with
a 70-84 record. Hank, who'd hit his first All-
Star homer the year before against Vida
Blue, hit another at the '72 game in his home
park. "That homer is one of the most dra-
matic I've ever hit. It is one of my greatest
thrills because it came in front of the Atlanta fans."

Hank is sure of one thing: he'll hang up
his spikes for good before his play ever gets

to the point where he is ashamed of it. "I feel I owe it to myself," he says. "I've had too good a career and played too long to go out and embarrass myself by hitting, say .250 and maybe hitting ten or twelve home runs. I have too much respect for the game of baseball to do that."

Hank expects that his bat will eventually get slower. Even now, he says, he gets tired a little quicker than he used to, and when he's tired — especially on one of those West Coast trips — his bat is slower, and he fouls off pitches he should hit. "It's frustrating," he admits, "but a couple of days' rest and I'm all right again."

He doubts that his reflexes are as quick as they were when he was in his early twenties or that he can circle the bases as fast, but his experience compensates. For instance, "I can go from first to third on any kind of single because I know the opposing outfielders and how they throw."

Meanwhile, Hank continues to give his all, no matter how he may feel. "When I get out on the field, I drive myself as hard as when I first started playing."

18

After the Game's Over

WHAT does Hank plan to do when he retires? One question he's been asked is, Would he want a manager's job? He has long thought that baseball should offer jobs as managers, or general managers, to blacks. He has said of baseball — the first of the sports to integrate — that "If you ride in the front of the bus, so to speak, sixteen or seventeen years and when you stop playing they have no place for you, and you go to the back again, then I don't think baseball has done anything for you."

Hank has also pointed to a group of managers who constantly have losing teams, but keep getting hired. "I think it's time they gave some black players a chance to do the same. Some of us would probably have done better," he has quipped.

Henry can think of several possible choices for black managers. There's Bill White, whom Hank knew as a player with the Cardinals, Phillies, and Giants: "He got along with everybody, no matter who it was. It seemed he had the respect of all his teammates." Then there's Maury Wills, "who stayed in the minor leagues so long he had to learn how to bunt, how to steal, how to figure the pitcher's moves."

The same holds true for Junior Gilliam, Hank's third recommendation. "These guys weren't as naturally gifted as some players, but they were great. They had to study the game more than others and they picked up more knowledge." Mays and Banks are also good prospects in Hank's opinion.

But would Hank himself want a manager's job?

Hank says, "I suppose after you've stayed in the game as long as I have, it's natural to have some desire to be a manager. You have your own ideas, how you'd like it played in a given situation, but right now, I just want to go out and play, feeling I'm part of the team."

Whether or not Hank would take a managing job after his playing days are over, it seems certain he'd welcome a chance to consider it.

(Bill Bartholomay, the president of the Braves, has indicated Hank would be strongly considered for an important nonplaying job.)

Hank's brother and ex-Brave, Tommie, who once went four-for-four using Henry's bat, thinks Hank has excellent qualifications to be a big-league manager. "He's the type of guy everyone respects. He knows a lot about the game and gets along with everyone," said Tommie.

Tommie, six years younger than Hank, had relatively little contact with him when they were children. But in the majors, he's had the benefit of his brother's advice. Once, for example, when he was at the plate, and Henry was on third, Hank yelled to him that he was jerking his head when he swung. And when Tommie first came up to the Braves, Hank would tell him what the different pitchers threw. "It helped me quite a bit," Tommie commented.

There's no question that Hank will be elected to baseball's Hall of Fame at Cooperstown, New York. It's just a matter of time. A player can't be elected to the Hall of Fame until he's been retired as a player for at least five years. Naturally, Hank looks forward to joining the club of baseball's greatest. "Just being mentioned as a future prospect is a great honor," he says.

When Henry does retire, he'll be able to devote more time to hunting and fishing, two of his favorite forms of relaxation. He likes golfing, too, though he emphasizes he's in a far different league as a golf-club swinger than golfer Tommy Aaron (no relation). If he were a particularly talented golfer, "I wouldn't be up there trying to hit a curve ball," Hank says, flashing his ready grin.

Retirement may give Hank more time to work for civil rights and other causes. In 1966 he traveled to Vietnam with Joe Torre, Stan Musial, Brooks Robinson, Harmon Killebrew, and sportscaster Mel Allen to talk to U.S. servicemen and answer their sports questions. Hank wasted little time making up his mind about going on the tour. He thanked the man who invited him, asked for the schedule, and got ready. "It's a trip everyone should make," Hank says, recalling how shocked he was at the poverty he found in the productive country that has been a battleground for so many years.

Though he could probably be elected to just about any office on the basis of his popularity, Hank rules out a political career for himself. In 1968, though, he was planning to campaign for the late Senator Robert F. Kennedy.

As might be expected, many of his friends are sports celebrities. In Wisconsin he knew all the Green Bay Packers — the late Vince Lombardi was a good friend — and he knows a good many of the Atlanta Falcons and Hawks. Jim Brown and Muhammad Ali are Henry's friends, as are Bill Bartholomay and John Quinn, the former Braves' general manager. He also has some show business acquaintances that include Doris Day and Chuck Connors.

Hank enjoys movies (though he shudders at the way actors swing bats in baseball films) and Broadway shows, and such TV programs as *The FBI* and *Mission Impossible*.

Hank is an excellent chef who delights in cooking seafood, steak, and his own special brand of Swedish meatballs. In Milwaukee the Aarons rented a house that had a patio laid out like a ballfield and a barbecue pit shaped like home plate. Hank enjoyed having cookouts there.

He met his wife when he was with the team in Jacksonville. They were married seven months later. The Aarons now have four children: Gail, Henry, Jr. ("Hankie"), Larry, and Dorinda, who was born on the same day as her father, February 5.

Hank, Sr., will have an occasional catch with his sons, who also love sports. The boys will even skip breakfast to play, unlike their father. When he was a boy, the only thing he'd stop playing baseball for was a meal.

The boys seem to take their father's fame in stride. Once, when a youngster was chasing Hank for an autograph, one of the boys asked, "For what?" Barbara Aaron got back at her son when he asked permission to go see two other prominent athletes who were in town. "For what?" she asked.

When Hank started playing baseball, he vowed his children would have more material comforts than he had as a child. So, among other things, they own minibikes and get generous-sized allowances. But Hank also wants his children to appreciate what they get and not be wasteful.

Of all the things he wants to give his children, however, the most important is education. Hank counts seeing two of his sisters graduated from college among the happiest moments of his life (outside of baseball). He helped them through financially.

His greatest joy comes: "Every time I look at my kids and see them growing up, see how large they're getting, see them playing sports, competing. Those are probably the happiest moments you can ask for."

Decisions about the careers that the Aaron children want to follow are being left up to them. Hank believes strongly that baseball with its good pay, pension plans, and the opportunity to see the country makes it hard to beat.

If Hank hadn't made it as an athlete, he probably would have become a teacher, though it's hard for him to say because baseball is all he's ever really known.

"I was lucky," he says. "I was good enough to get to the big leagues and stay there." But not everybody is that fortunate — or talented. And that's why he tells his younger brother James, who is in college and anxious to get out and play: "Finish school first. You'll only be about twenty-three, and you'll still have a lot of time to play. And in case you don't make it, you'll have something to fall back on."

In baseball or anything else, Hank is convinced that everyone — rich or poor, bright or average, black or white — can make worthwhile achievements, providing he appreciates his opportunities and abilities, and works toward his goal.

"Some people believe that because they're poor, they'll never get any place. But just because you're from a poor family doesn't mean you always have to be poor. If a kid has any talent — and I believe God's given us all *some* talent — he can make a contribution. Every kid can, and it doesn't matter whether he's white, black, or blue.

"But," Hank cautions, "nobody's going to hand it to you. You can't just sit back; you've got to work for it. And there's always room for improvement."

This has been Hank Aaron's watchword throughout his career — from the days he had a friend take movies of his batting technique so he could study and improve it, until today. It's a safe bet that Hammerin' Hank, one of the greatest who ever put wood to horsehide, will keep looking for ways to improve on his near perfection until the sad day when he hangs up Number 44 for the last time.

DWIGHT HOWARD

His whiplash wrists and intense concentration combine to
help make Hank Aaron one of the greatest hitters of all time.

HANK AARON'S RECORD

Born on February 5, 1934, in Mobile, Alabama. Height,
6 ft. Weight, 180 pounds. Bats right. Throws right.

Year	Club	Pos	G	AB	R	H	TB	2B	3B	HR	RBI	SB	BA
1952	Eau Claire	SS	87	345	79	116	170	19	4	9	61	25	.336
1953	Jacksonville	2B-OF	137	574	*115	*208	*338	*36	14	22	*125	13	*.362
1954	Milwaukee	OF	122	468	58	131	209	27	6	13	69	2	.280
1955	Milwaukee	OF-2B	153	602	105	189	325	*37	9	27	106	3	.314
1956	Milwaukee	OF	153	609	106	*200	*340	*34	14	26	92	2	*.328
1957	Milwaukee	OF	151	615	*118	198	*369	27	6	*44	*132	1	.322
1958	Milwaukee	OF	153	601	109	196	328	34	4	30	95	4	.326
1959	Milwaukee	OF-3B	154	629	116	*223	*400	46	7	39	123	8	*.355
1960	Milwaukee	OF-2B	153	590	102	172	334	20	11	40	*126	16	.292
1961	Milwaukee	OF-3B	*155	603	115	197	358	*39	10	34	120	21	.327
1962	Milwaukee	OF-1B	156	592	127	191	366	28	6	-45	128	15	.323
1963	Milwaukee	OF	161	631	*121	201	*370	29	4	•44	*130	31	.319
1964	Milwaukee	OF-2B	145	570	103	187	293	30	2	24	95	22	.328
1965	Milwaukee	OF	150	570	109	181	319	•40	1	32	89	24	.318
1966	Atlanta	OF-2B	158	603	117	168	325	23	1	*44	*127	21	.279
1967	Atlanta	OF-2B	155	600	•113	184	344	37	3	*39	109	17	.307
1968	Atlanta	OF-1B	160	606	84	174	302	33	4	29	86	28	.287
1969	Atlanta	OF-1B	147	547	100	164	*332	30	3	44	97	9	.300
1970	Atlanta	OF-1B-3B	150	516-	103	154	296	26	1	38	118	9	.298
Major-League Totals			2576	9952	1806	3110	5610	540	92	592	1842	233	.313

* — Denotes led league.
• — Tied for league lead.

World Series Record

Year	Club	Pos	G	AB	R	H	TB	2B	3B	HR	RBI	SB	BA
1957	Milwaukee	OF	7	28	5	11	22	0	1	3	7	0	.393
1958	Milwaukee	OF	7	27	3	9	11	2	0	0	2	0	.333
World Series Totals			14	55	8	20	33	2	1	3	9	0	.364

Championship Series Record

Year	Club	Pos	G	AB	R	H	TB	2B	3B	HR	RBI	SB	BA
1969	Atlanta	OF	3	14	3	5	16	2	0	3	7	0	.357

All-Star Game Record

Year	Club	Pos	G	AB	R	H	TB	2B	3B	HR	RBI	SB	BA
1955	National	OF	1	2	1	2	2	0	0	0	1	0	1.000
1956	National	OF	1	1	0	0	0	0	0	0	0	0	.000
1957	National	OF	1	4	0	1	1	0	0	0	0	0	.250
1958	National	OF	1	2	0	0	0	0	0	0	1	0	.000
1959	National	OF	2	7	1	2	0	0	0	0	2	0	.286
1960	National	OF	2	7	0	0	0	0	0	0	0	0	.000
1961	National	PH-OF	2	3	1	1	1	0	0	0	0	0	.333
1962	National*	OF	1	2	0	0	0	0	0	0	0	0	.000
1963	National	OF	1	4	1	0	0	0	0	0	0	0	.000
1964	National	PH	1	1	0	0	0	0	0	0	0	0	.000
1965	National	OF	1	5	0	1	1	0	0	0	0	0	.200
1966	National	OF	1	4	0	0	0	0	0	0	0	0	.000
1967	National	OF	1	6	0	1	1	0	0	0	0	1	.167
1968	National	OF	1	3	0	1	1	0	0	0	0	1	.333
1969	National	OF	1	4	1	1	1	0	0	0	0	0	.250
1970	National	OF	1	2	0	0	0	0	0	0	0	0	.000
All-Star Games Totals			19	57	5	10	8	0	0	0	4	2	.175

* — Named to National League All-Star team (first game); replaced because of ankle injury.

Additional Batting and Fielding Figures

Year	Club	CS	SH	SF	TOT BB	INT BB	HP	SO	GI DP	SLG AVG	PO	A	E	FLD AVG
1954	Mil	2	6	4	28	0	3	39	13	.447	223	5	7	.970
1955	Mil	1	7	4	49	5	3	61	20	.540	340	93	15	.967
1956	Mil	4	5	7	37	6	2	54	21	.558	316	17	13	.962
1957	Mil	1	0	3	57	15	0	58	13	.600	346	9	6	.983
1958	Mil	1	0	3	59	16	1	49	21	.546	305	12	5	.984
1959	Mil	0	0	9	51	17	4	54	19	.636	263	22	5	.983
1960	Mil	7	0	12	60	13	2	63	8	.556	321	13	6	.982
1961	Mil	9	1	9	56	20	2	64	16	.594	379	15	7	.982
1962	Mil	7	0	6	66	14	3	73	14	.618	341	11	7	.980
1963	Mil	5	0	5	78	18	0	94	11	.586	267	10	6	.979
1964	Mil	4	0	2	62	9	0	46	22	.514	284	28	6	.981
1965	Mil	4	0	8	60	10	1	81	15	.560	298	9	4	.987
1966	Atl	3	0	8	76	15	1	96	14	.539	315	12	4	.988
1967	Atl	6	0	6	63	19	0	97	11	.573	322	12	7	.979
1968	Atl	5	0	5	64	23	1	62	21	.498	418	20	5	.989
1969	Atl	10	0	3	87	19	2	47	14	.607	299	13	5	.984
1970	Atl	0	0	6	74	15	2	63	13	.574	319	10	7	.979
1971	Atl	1	0	5	71	21	2	58	9	.669	733	40	5	.993
1972	Atl	0	0	2	92	15	1	55	17	.514	996	70	17	.984
Totals		70	19	107	1,190	270	30	1,214	292	.566	7085	421	137	.982